항공운송 실무영어

【 Practical English for Cabin Crew 】

최 경 옥 지음

14   정답 ③

〈매출채권〉

기초	50,000	기중회수	60,000
		대손확정	30,000
당기외상매출액	80,000	기말	40,000
	130,000		130,000

15   정답 ③

- 20X1년 말 회수가능액 : Max[120,000, 100,000] = 120,000
- 20X2년 7월 1일 감가상각비 : $\dfrac{120,000}{4} \times \dfrac{6}{12} = 15,000$
- 20X2년 7월 1일 장부가액 : 120,000 − 15,000 = 105,000
- 유형자산처분손익 : 90,000 − 105,000 = 15,000 손실

16   정답 ③

- 재고액 : 200,000 − 30,000 = 170,000
- 실지재고수량 × 1,000 = 170,000 → 실지재고수량 = 170

17   정답 ④

- 1월 말 재공품원가(A) : (A × 80%) + 2,000,000 = 1,940,000 + A → A = 300,000
- 직접노무원가 : 300,000 × 60% = 180,000
- 직접재료원가(B) : B + 180,000 + (B × 40%) = 2,000,000 → B = 1,300,000

18   정답 ③

- 단위당 변동원가 : $\dfrac{30,000}{200} = 150$
- 고정원가 : 30,000 − (150 × 100) = 15,000
- 총제품제조원가 : {500 × (150 × 80%)} + (15,000 × 1.1) = 76,500

19   정답 ④

$(5,000 - 3,000) \times 판매량 = 500,000 + \dfrac{120,000}{1 - 40\%}$ → 판매량 = 350

20   정답 ③

- 완성품환산량 : (800 × 100%) + (200 × 50%) = 900
- 완성품환산량 단위당 원가 : $\dfrac{3,000 + 42,000}{900} = 50$
- 기말재공품원가 : (200 × 50%) × 50 = 5,000

공기업 회계학

제20회 최종모의고사 정답 및 해설

01	02	03	04	05	06	07	08	09	10	11	12	13	14	15	16	17	18	19	20
⑤	①	①	②	②	②	⑤	②	④	③	⑤	①	②	②	④	④	②	①	⑤	③

01 정답 ⑤
자가사용부동산이 아니라 투자부동산으로 분류한다.

02 정답 ①
$110,000 - 10,000 + 10,000 + 5,000(하역료) - 5,000(매입할인) - 2,000 + 500 = 108,500$

03 정답 ①
- 순매입액 : $20,000 + 2,000 - 1,000 - 600 - 400 = 20,000$
- 매출원가 : $10,000 + 20,000 - 12,000 = 18,000$
- 순매출액 : $27,000 - 1,800 - 1,200 - 500 = 23,500$
- 매출총이익 : $23,500 - 18,000 = 5,500$
- 영업이익 : $5,500 - 2,500 - 1,000 = 2,000$

04 정답 ②
재무제표의 표시통화를 천 단위나 백만 단위로 표시할 때 이해 가능성이 제고될 수 있다.

05 정답 ②
시험 과정에서 생산된 재화의 순매각금액과 재배치·재편성 과정에서 발생하는 원가는 모두 당기손익으로 처리한다.

06 정답 ②
거래가격은 고객에게 약속한 재화나 용역을 이전하고 그 대가로 기업이 받을 권리를 갖게 될 것으로 예상하는 금액이며, 제3자를 대신해서 회수한 금액은 제외된다.

Preface

Welcome to ***Practical English for Cabin Crew***, a textbook designed to equip future flight attendants with the English communication skills essential for delivering professional, safe, and customer-focused service on board.

As international air travel continues to grow, English has become the global language of aviation. Cabin crew members are expected not only to ensure passenger comfort but also to manage a wide range of in-flight situations with clear and confident communication. This textbook was created with that purpose in mind — to help learners develop both the language and the situational awareness required for success in this fast-paced industry.

The content of this book is organized according to the phases of flight, guiding students through realistic tasks and dialogues from pre-flight briefing to post-flight duties. Each unit features:

- Learning objectives for practical skill development
- Thematic vocabulary and expressions commonly used in aviation
- Realistic dialogues and role-play activities
- Comprehension checks and wrap-up quizzes for self-assessment

Special attention has been given to role-play and scenario-based learning, encouraging students to build confidence by simulating real in-flight situations, such as handling service disruptions, making announcements, assisting passengers, and managing emergencies — all in English.

This book is ideal for use in university-level aviation English classes, airline training programs, or individual preparation for cabin crew interviews. Whether you are just beginning your journey or preparing to take flight in your career, we hope this textbook helps you soar toward your goals with confidence, professionalism, and poise.

Thank you for choosing English for Cabin Crew.

We wish you a safe and successful journey ahead.

Introduction

Welcome to English for Cabin Crew!

This course is specifically designed for students who dream of becoming professional cabin crew members. In the airline industry, flight attendants are not only responsible for ensuring safety and comfort but also serve as ambassadors of the airline. To succeed in this highly globalized field, strong English communication skills are essential.

Why English Matters in the Skies

English is the international language of aviation. Cabin crew must be able to communicate clearly with passengers from different countries, relay information to the cockpit, and collaborate with ground staff and colleagues all in English. Whether giving safety announcements, handling in-flight service, or managing unexpected situations, effective communication in English is a key part of delivering excellent service.

What You Will Learn

This course helps you build the essential language skills and professional mindset needed for a successful career as a cabin crew member. You will:

- **Master Cabin Crew Vocabulary**

    Learn aviation-related words and phrases used in service, safety, and emergency situations.

- **Practice Real-Life Scenarios**

    Build confidence through dialogues and role-plays based on actual in-flight situations.

- **Improve Speaking and Listening Skills**

    Practice responding appropriately to announcements, requests, and passenger needs.

- **Develop Polished Service Language**

    Learn how to speak politely, resolve problems calmly, and show empathy — the heart of excellent customer service.

Course Structure

This book is organized according to the three main phases of flight:
1. Before Take-Off
    Pre-flight briefing, cabin preparation, boarding procedures, and announcements
2. During the Flight
    In-flight service, handling passenger requests, managing safety and medical issues
3. After Landing
    Arrival procedures, farewell communication, and post-flight duties

Each unit includes essential vocabulary, practical expressions, situation-based dialogues, comprehension checks, and role-play activities to help you build both language proficiency and professional competence.

Whether you are preparing for a cabin crew interview, training for your first airline position, or simply looking to improve your aviation English, this course is your step-by-step guide to taking off with confidence.

How to Use This Book

This textbook is designed to help aspiring cabin crew members develop practical English communication skills aligned with real in-flight duties and phases of flight. To make the most of this book, please follow the structure and learning flow presented in each unit.

Unit Structure Overview

Each unit is organized in the following format:

1. Learning Objectives

Clear goals are set at the beginning of each unit to focus your learning and skill development.

2. Introduction

A short explanation of the topic introduces its real-life context and relevance to the cabin crew role.

3. Key Vocabulary

Essential words and terms used in cabin crew communication are introduced with simple definitions.

4. Useful Expressions

Phrases commonly used in flight operations are provided to enhance fluency and confidence in conversations.

5. Warm-up Quiz / Exercises

These short activities activate prior knowledge and introduce key terms in a fun and engaging way.

6. Dialogue Practice

Realistic conversations simulate typical cabin crew scenarios, such as boarding, in-flight service, safety announcements, and problem-solving. Each dialogue includes:

- Setting: Where and when the dialogue takes place
- Characters: Roles of the speakers (e.g. Flight Attendant, Passenger)
- Dialogue: Authentic English exchanges
- Key Vocabulary: Important words used in the conversation
- Alternative Expressions: Other ways to say similar things

7. Comprehension Check
Multiple-choice or short-answer questions help review the key points of the dialogues and vocabulary.

8. Role-play Activity Worksheet
Learners work in pairs or small groups to act out real-life scenarios, using the expressions and vocabulary learned.

9. Wrap-up Quiz
A final review quiz reinforces the learning in each unit and checks vocabulary, grammar, and practical use.

Tips for Learners
- Practice aloud: Repeat vocabulary and expressions to improve pronunciation and fluency.
- Use role-plays actively: Don't be afraid to perform. Use gestures and body language to simulate real cabin crew behavior.
- Create your own dialogues: Try modifying the examples or making up new ones based on your own experience.
- Review regularly: Revisit vocabulary lists and quizzes before moving on to the next unit.
- Record yourself: Listening to your own speaking can help you correct pronunciation and intonation.

Tips for Instructors
- Encourage pair and group work for role-play sessions.
- Use the dialogues to model tone, register, and professional communication styles.
- Supplement with real airline announcements or safety videos when available.
- Provide feedback on both language use and customer service attitude.
- Assign wrap-up quizzes or comprehension checks as formative assessments.

Table of Contents

Part 1 Before Take-off

Unit	Title	Description	Page
Unit 1	Pre-Flight Briefing	Cabin crew meeting before the flight: safety, service, coordination	5
Unit 2	Cabin Preparation	Equipment checks, Galley setup, Safety and security checks, Cabin readiness	15
Unit 3	Boarding Procedures	Greeting passengers, verifying boarding passes, seat guidance	29
Unit 4	Seating Arrangement	Assisting with wrong seats, seat swaps, special requests	41
Unit 5	Pre-Departure Announcements & Checks	Safety demos, final cabin checks, securing the cabin, door arming	55

Part 2 After Take-off

Unit	Title	Description	Page
Unit 6	In-flight Service Preparation	Trolley setup, meal & beverage planning, coordination	73
Unit 7	Meal & Beverage Service	Taking orders, serving, handling special meal requests	83
Unit 8	Dealing with Passenger Requests	Answering calls, providing blankets, helping with devices	101
Unit 9	Handling In-flight Issues	Medical emergencies, unruly passengers, turbulence handling	115

Part 3 After Landing

Unit	Title	Description	Page
Unit 10	Preparing for Landing	Final cabin check, announcement scripts, seatbelt check	131
Unit 11	Arrival Procedures	Farewell greetings, assisting disembarkation, transit passengers	145
Unit 12	Post-Flight Duties & Debriefing	Cabin check, lost items, crew debriefing, reporting issues	157

항공운송 실무영어
【 Practical English for Cabin Crew 】

에듀컨텐츠·휴피아
CH Educontents·Huepia

Part i

Before Take-off

Unit 01. The Pre-Flight Briefing
Unit 02. Cabin Preparation
Unit 03. Passenger Boarding & Greeting
Unit 04. Handling carry-on baggage and special handling passengers
Unit 05. Pre-Departure Announcements & Checks

에듀컨텐츠 휴피아
CH Educontents Huepia

UNIT 01. The Pre-Flight Briefing

Lesson objectives

- Understand the Purpose of Pre-flight Briefing
- Identify Key Components of a Pre-flight Briefing

Introduction

A pre-flight briefing is a meeting held before a flight between the flight crew (pilots and flight attendants) to review important information, roles, and responsibilities specific to the upcoming flight. This briefing helps ensure that everyone on the crew is prepared and coordinated to handle various scenarios, prioritize passenger safety, and provide consistent service. A pre-flight briefing is essential for the flight crew to ensure safety, efficiency, and high-quality service on every flight.

Key Components of a Pre-Flight Briefing

1. Flight Details and Schedule
Information on the flight route, expected weather conditions, flight duration, and any potential delays.

2. Passenger Information
Overview of the passenger list, especially noting any special handling passengers, such as those requiring wheelchairs, unaccompanied minors, or passengers with other needs.

3. Safety and Emergency Procedures
Review of emergency exits, equipment functionality, and each crew member's role in case of an emergency. It also includes reminders about handling turbulence or other potential in-flight disruptions.

4. Service Coordination

Planning the timing and delivery of in-flight services, such as meal and beverage service, duty-free sales, and entertainment management.

5. Communication Protocol

Guidelines on communication between cabin crew and cockpit crew for any updates or situations that may arise during the flight.

Crew Briefing

A pilot and cabin crew briefing is a coordinated pre-flight meeting between the flight deck crew (pilots) and the cabin crew to ensure that all team members are aligned on the details of the upcoming flight. This briefing is critical for maintaining safety, preparing for any unique flight circumstances, and ensuring a seamless experience for passengers.

Purpose of the Briefing

- **Safety Coordination**

The primary purpose is to review safety procedures and assign roles in case of an emergency.
Ensures that all crew members understand the chain of command and emergency protocols.

- **Flight-Specific Information**

Provides details about the flight route, weather conditions, potential turbulence, and expected flight time.
Highlights any special circumstances, such as medical emergencies, VIP passengers, or operational changes.

- **Crew Communication**

Establishes clear communication protocols between the cockpit and cabin crew.

Ensures that both teams can quickly share updates during the flight.

- **Passenger Service Preparation**

Aligns cabin crew on in-flight service flow, including meal timings, duty-free sales, and entertainment management.
Reviews any special handling passengers and their specific needs.

Topics Covered in the Briefing

By the Pilot (Flight Deck Crew)
1. Flight details: Departure and arrival airports, flight duration, cruising altitude, and expected weather.
2. Safety concerns: Turbulence, alternate landing plans, or any technical considerations.
3. Emergency communication: How and when the cabin crew should notify the cockpit of an issue.

By the Lead Cabin Crew (Purser/Lead Flight Attendant)
1. Cabin safety: Verifying emergency equipment and exit doors.
2. Passenger care: Assigning roles for special handling passengers (e.g. wheelchair users, unaccompanied minors).
3. Service coordination: Planning the sequence and timing of meal and beverage services.
4. Crew roles: Assigning specific responsibilities to each cabin crew member for both routine and emergency situations.

Why the Briefing is Important

- **Team Alignment**

It ensures all crew members are aware of their roles and responsibilities, creating a coordinated team environment.

- **Preparedness**

Reviewing flight-specific details and potential challenges ensures that the crew is ready to handle any situation calmly and efficiently.

- **Passenger Experience**

Proper preparation allows the crew to deliver a smooth, safe, and enjoyable flight experience.

- **Safety Assurance**

Aligning on emergency procedures reduces the risk of miscommunication or delays during critical moments.

Warm-up exercise

A. Look at the pictures and the words. In your groups or with your partner, discuss what you usually bring on an airplane. What do you need to bring on an airplane? Choose from the words below.

- ☐ Passport
- ☐ MP3 player
- ☐ Books
- ☐ Credit cards
- ☐ Amenity kit
- ☐ Crew IDs
- ☐ Extra clothes
- ☐ Spare uniforms

B. With your partner, discuss which of these things are usually mentioned in the pre-flight briefing, and why.

teamwork	leadership
introductions	weather
meals service	special needs passengers
emergency procedures	clear task allocation
safety	responsibilities
motivation	personal appearance

Word & Phrases

Complete the sentences below using the words given in the box.

briefing	passenger manifest
emergency exit	special handling passengers
flight details	safety equipment
cabin crew	flight crew
turbulence	crew coordination

1. _____ lists all passengers, including those needing extra help.
2. The captain shares _____, such as the flight time and weather.
3. _____, like those in wheelchairs, need extra care from the crew.
4. As a _____, you help passengers and handle any problems during the flight.
5. The _____ tell the crew about flight conditions and any special needs.
6. Good _____ is important for a safe and smooth flight.
7. The crew has a _____ before every flight to go over safety and passenger details.
8. Flight attendants must check that _____ are clear before takeoff.
9. Checking _____, like life vests and oxygen masks, is important before the flight.
10. During _____, passengers should keep their seat belts on.

• 항공운송 실무영어 Practical English for Cabin Crew

Briefing scenarios

Crew Briefing-A flight with special handling passengers	
Flight Details	• Flight Number: CW123 • Sector: Incheon(ICN)-Shanghai(PVG) • Expected flight time: 2 hours and 30 minutes • Aircraft type: B737-900ER • Configuration: FC(8) / EY(165) • Weather: Mild turbulence expected during descent • Special passengers: 1 wheelchair, 2 unaccompanied minors
Crew Information & Roles	• Captain: David Kim • First Officer: Jane Thompson • Lead Cabin Crew(Purser): Sarah Lee • Flight Attendant 1: Kevin Tran(Assigned to assist visually impaired passenger) • Flight Attendant 2: Olivia White(Responsible for mid cabin service and general assistance) • Flight Attendant 3: Priya Nair(Overseeing meal service and allergy management
Safety & Service Procedures	Safety Procedures • Pre-Flight Safety Checks • Passenger Safety Briefing • Turbulence Protocols • Emergency Preparedness Service Procedures • Pre-takeoff Service • In-Flight Service • Beverage & Meal Services • Duty-free sales Special Passenger Assistance Pre-Landing Service

Pre-flight Briefing

1. Flight Information
Captain:
Good afternoon, everyone. Boarding will begin in about five minutes, so let's start our briefing.
Today's flight time is about 52 minutes. There may be some strong winds during takeoff, so please remain seated until I inform you it is safe to begin the service.
First Officer:
If we expect turbulence during the flight, I will update you right away. Also, if you notice any problems in the cabin, especially safety-related, please let us know immediately. Don't wait until after 10,000 feet. Your input is always important.

2. Cabin Responsibilities
Purser (Lead Cabin Crew):
Thank you, Captain. For the cabin side: Bobby will brief the emergency exit rows. Please make sure the overhead bins near emergency equipment remain clear. I will double-check the emergency equipment before boarding.
Flight Attendant 1:
Understood.

3. Special Information
Purser:
The gate agent informed us that a law enforcement officer will be traveling with a prisoner. Captain, would you like us to notify you when they board?
Captain:
Yes, please let me know. Thank you.

4. Communication & Cockpit Access
Flight Attendant 2:
Captain, how should we enter the cockpit during the flight?
Captain:
Just use your key. If there's any issue, call us on the interphone first.

5. Final Remarks
Captain:
Thank you, everyone. Let's work together for a safe and smooth flight. Any

•항공운송 실무영어 Practical English for Cabin Crew

questions before we start boarding?
All Cabin Crew Members
No questions. Thank you, Captain.

Flight crew briefing to flight attendants

Group Work 1

From now on, you will create a virtual flight scenario. After that, complete a script for role-playing the pre-flight briefing on the next page.

	Crew Briefing-A flight with special handling passengers
Flight Details	• Flight Number: • Sector: • Expected flight time: • Aircraft type: • Configuration: FC(　　) / EY(　　) • Weather: • Special passengers:
Crew Information & Roles	• Captain: • First Officer: • Lead Cabin Crew(Purser): • Flight Attendant 1: • Flight Attendant 2: • Flight Attendant 3:
Safety & Service Procedures	Safety Procedures • Pre-Flight Safety Checks • Passenger Safety Briefing • Turbulence Protocols • Emergency Preparedness Service Procedures • Pre-takeoff Service • In-Flight Service

Unit 01. The Pre-Flight Briefing

	• Beverage & Meal Services
	• Duty-free sales
	Special Passenger Assistance
	Pre-Landing Service

Group Work 2

Instructions:

Work in groups of 3-4. Assign roles (CCI and FAs). Use the dialogue and expressions from the unit to conduct a pre-flight briefing. Discuss aircraft type, weather, special passengers, and service plan.

Role-play Scenarios (choose one):

1. Flight to Tokyo with two UMs and expected turbulence.
2. Flight to Sydney with a malfunctioning galley and delayed catering.
3. Flight to Manila with a VIP and PRM onboard.

Checklist:

- Greet and assign positions
- Share flight details and weather
- Mention special passengers
- Review service plan
- Discuss safety and security reminders

에듀컨텐츠·휴피아
CH Educontents Huepia

UNIT 02. Cabin Preparation

Lesson objectives

By the end of this unit, students will be able to:
- Identify and describe the key tasks involved in cabin preparation before take-off.
- Use appropriate English expressions for reporting equipment status and galley readiness.
- Practice dialogue for checking cabin safety, arming doors, and preparing for boarding.
- Apply standard procedures for communicating safety readiness in English.

Preparation for Boarding

Pre-flight preparation for boarding refers to the tasks and procedures carried out by airline staff, especially cabin crew, to ensure that the aircraft is ready for passengers to board safely and efficiently.
These tasks typically include:

1. Checking passenger information and seating arrangements.
2. Inspecting the cabin for cleanliness and readiness.
3. Verifying safety equipment is in place and functioning.
4. Coordinating with ground staff for special assistance needs.
5. Reviewing safety and emergency procedures.

Safety Checks

A safety check involves verifying that all equipment, systems, and procedures are properly in place to ensure the physical safety of passengers, crew, and the aircraft. It focuses on minimizing risks related to accidents or emergencies.

Examples of Safety Checks

Emergency Equipment Inspection:
- Confirm that fire extinguishers, life vests, oxygen masks, and first aid kits are present and functional.

Seatbelt and Seat Readiness:
- Check that seat belts are functional and seats are properly positioned (e.g., tray tables stowed, seat backs upright).

Cabin Environment:
- Ensure overhead bins are securely closed and no items are at risk of falling.
- Verify that the cabin floor is free of obstructions or hazards.

Door and Slide Readiness:
- Check that doors are armed/disarmed as required and evacuation slides are functional.

Lavatory Checks:
- Examine lavatories for prohibited items or evidence of tampering.

Galley Check:
- Inspect galley areas for any unauthorized items, tampering with equipment, or potential security risks.

Cockpit Security:
- Verify that access to the cockpit is restricted and secure.

Safety checks before boarding

Security Checks

A security check involves a thorough inspection of the cabin, galleys, lavatories, and storage areas before passengers are allowed to board. The purpose is to ensure that no prohibited items, suspicious objects, or evidence of tampering are present, and that the aircraft is secure and ready for boarding.

Examples of Security Checks

Cabin Area
- Inspect all seat pockets for suspicious or prohibited items (e.g. sharp objects, liquids, dangerous goods).
- Check under seats and in overhead bins for unattended bags or unusual items.
- Ensure that safety information cards and life vests are in place and undisturbed.

Lavatories
- Confirm that no prohibited or suspicious items are hidden in waste bins, storage compartments, or behind mirrors.
- Check smoke detectors for tampering.

Galley Area
- Inspect galley carts, storage compartments, and ovens for unauthorized items or suspicious modifications.
- Verify that catering seals are intact and show no signs of tampering.

Storage Compartments & Crew Areas
- Examine closets, jump seats, and other crew storage spaces for unusual or prohibited items.
- Check emergency equipment storage for unauthorized objects.

Doors and Exits
- Confirm that access panels, doors, and emergency exits show no evidence of tampering.
- Ensure that security seals, if applicable, are intact.

Cockpit Access
- Verify that cockpit door locks and security systems are functional.
- Confirm that no unauthorized items are left near the cockpit entrance.

Note for Cabin Crew:
Security checks must be conducted systematically and documented according to company procedures. Any suspicious finding must be reported to the Purser and Captain immediately before passenger boarding begins.

Pre-Flight Checks (Safety checks)

Key Vocabulary

Word	Meaning
safety check	verification that equipment, seats, and procedures meet safety standards.
security check	inspection to ensure no prohibited or suspicious items are on board.
emergency equipment	devices such as fire extinguishers, oxygen masks, and life vests used in emergencies.
galley readiness	ensuring the kitchen area is clean, secure, and stocked properly.
catering seal	a security seal placed on galley carts and compartments to prevent tampering.
cockpit access	controlled entry to the flight deck, restricted for security reasons.
lavatory check	inspection of lavatories for cleanliness, hidden items, or tampering.
suspicious item	an object that may be dangerous or unauthorized on board.
tampering	interfering with or damaging equipment, seals, or safety systems.

Unit 02. Cabin Preparation

Useful expressions

1. Excuse me, could you tell me your name, please?
2. The weather today is expected to be smooth.
3. Our main priority is safety.
4. Today's service is include snacks, meals, and drinks.
5. Can I just check what the flight time is?
6. Can I clarify the cockpit procedures?
7. Does anyone have questions about today's flight and
8. Procedures?
9. Please check that all emergency equipment in your area is ready and working.
10. Let's keep clear communication during the flight.

Warm-Up Quiz

Safety Equipment

Match the words with the pictures.

1. _____ fire extinguisher
2. _____ life vest
3. _____ oxygen bottle
4. _____ first aid kit
5. _____ AED (Automated External Defibrillator)

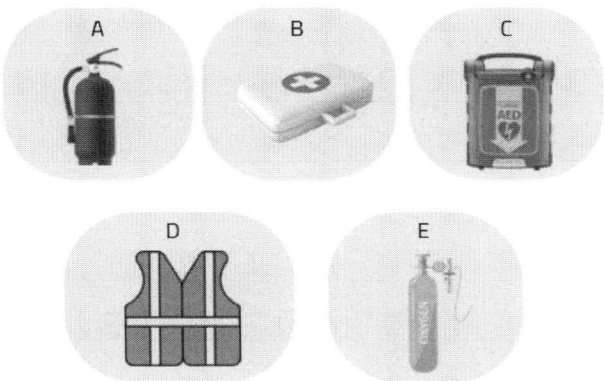

• 항공운송 실무영어 Practical English for Cabin Crew

Word & Phrases

Complete the sentences below using the words given in the view.

seat belts	suspicious
unauthorized	restricted area
overhead bin	aisle
lavatory	emergency exit
galley	emergency equipment

1. The cabin crew checked that all _____ were neatly placed and functional before passenger boarding.

2. The purser checked that the cockpit door, a _____ area, was locked and secure.

3. During their pre-boarding cabin inspection, the crew reported a _____ item left on a seat.

4. The crew inspected all _____ to confirm they were operational and unobstructed.

5. The flight attendant checked the _____ to ensure it was clean and stocked with toiletries.

6. The flight attendants ensured the _____ were clear of any obstructions to allow passengers to board safely.

7. The crew verified that all _____ equipment was properly stowed.

8. The crew confirmed that every seat had a _____ in the pocket.

9. The flight attendant checked that all _____ were empty.

10. The crew inspected all _____ , including fire extinguishers and oxygen bottles, before passenger boarding.

Unit 02. Cabin Preparation

Conversations

Situation 1: Galley Equipment Check

Setting:
This takes place in the front galley of the aircraft. Two cabin crew members are checking the galley before passengers board. They need to make sure the equipment is safe and ready for use.

Characters:
- Senior Cabin Crew
- Junior Cabin Crew

Dialogue

Senior Flight Attendant: Did you check the galley equipment?
Junior Flight Attendant: Yes. The ovens and coffee makers are working well.
Senior Flight Attendant: Are the galley carts locked?
Junior Flight Attendant: Yes, all the carts are locked and in place.
Senior Flight Attendant: Great. Don't forget to check the water boiler.
Junior Flight Attendant: Already checked. It's working fine.
Senior Flight Attendant: Perfect. Let's finish the report and get ready for boarding.

Key Vocabulary

Word	Meaning
galley	The kitchen area on an airplane
oven	Equipment used to heat food
coffee maker	A machine to make coffee
cart	A trolley that holds food and drinks
water boiler	A machine to heat water

Alternative Expressions

Original Expression	Alternative Expression
Working well	Okay / Fine
Locked and in place	Safe and ready
Let's finish the report	Let's complete the checklist
Don't forget to check the water boiler	Please remember to check the water boiler

• 항공운송 실무영어 Practical English for Cabin Crew

Situation 2: Emergency Equipment Verification

Setting:
During pre-boarding preparation, two cabin crew members are conducting a routine check of emergency equipment, such as fire extinguishers, oxygen bottles, and life vests. This is done before passengers board to ensure all items are in place and functioning.

Characters:
- Cabin Crew 1 (Senior)
- Cabin Crew 2 (Junior)

Dialogue

Cabin Crew 1: Let's start the emergency equipment check in the front galley.
Cabin Crew 2: Sure. The fire extinguisher is present and the pressure gauge is in the green zone.
Cabin Crew 1: Great. How about the oxygen bottle?
Cabin Crew 2: It's secured and showing 1600 psi. Mask and tubing are attached properly.
Cabin Crew 1: Perfect. Please confirm that the life vest is under the jump seat.
Cabin Crew 2: Yes, it's there and sealed.
Cabin Crew 1: Good. Repeat the same checks in the aft section and let me know if anything is missing or tampered with.
Cabin Crew 2: Will do. I'll report back in five minutes.

Key Vocabulary

Term	Meaning
fire extinguisher	A device used to put out small fires
oxygen bottle	Portable oxygen supply for emergencies
pressure gauge	Instrument showing pressure level
life vest	A personal flotation device used in emergencies
tampered with	Interfered with or altered, possibly unsafely

Unit 02. Cabin Preparation

Alternative Expressions

Original Expression	Alternative Expression
The pressure gauge is in the green zone.	The pressure level is normal.
Mask and tubing are attached properly.	Everything is connected as required.
Repeat the same checks in the aft section.	Please carry out identical checks at the rear.
I'll report back in five minutes.	I'll update you shortly.

Situation 3: Cabin Readiness & Seat Check

Setting:
Cabin crew are conducting final cabin readiness checks before passengers board. This includes inspecting seat belts, tray tables, overhead bins, and ensuring the cabin is clean and safe.

Characters:
- Cabin Crew 1
- Cabin Crew 2

Dialogue

Cabin Crew 1: Let's check the cabin seating area now.
Cabin Crew 2: Okay. Starting from row 1. Seat belts are unbuckled and visible.
Cabin Crew 1: Tray tables stowed, seat backs upright?
Cabin Crew 2: Yes, all are secured. Overhead bins are closed and nothing is sticking out.
Cabin Crew 1: Good. Let's make sure the aisle is clear and there are no personal items on the floor.
Cabin Crew 2: Aisle is clear. I picked up a small bag and placed it in the overhead bin.
Cabin Crew 1: Excellent. Once we finish the rear section, let's report cabin readiness to the Purser.
Cabin Crew 2: Understood. Ready to move to the next section.

• 항공운송 실무영어 Practical English for Cabin Crew

Key Vocabulary

Term	Meaning
tray table	A small foldable table in front of the passenger's seat
seat back upright	Seat positioned vertically as required for take-off
overhead bin	Storage compartment above the seats
aisle	The walkway between seat rows
cabin readiness	Condition where the cabin is safe and ready for passengers

Alternative Expressions

Original Expression	Alternative Expression
Tray tables stowed, seat backs upright?	Are the tray tables folded and seats in position?
Overhead bins are closed.	The compartments above are properly shut.
Aisle is clear.	The walkway is free from obstruction.
Let's report cabin readiness to the Purser.	We'll inform the Purser that the cabin is ready.

Situation 4: Boarding Clearance

Setting:
In the cockpit, shortly before boarding begins. The Purser enters the flight deck to give a final update on the cabin status and receive boarding clearance from the Flight Crew. Both parties confirm that all pre-boarding preparations are complete and the aircraft is safe for passenger boarding.

Characters:
- Purser
- Flight Crew(Captain)

Unit 02. Cabin Preparation

Dialogue

Purser: Good afternoon, Captain. The cabin is ready. All safety and security checks have been completed.
Captain: Thank you. Were there any issues reported by the cabin crew?
Purser: No, everything is in order. Emergency equipment is verified, the galley is secure, and the doors remain disarmed.
Captain: Excellent. Any special service passengers to be aware of?
Purser: Yes, we have two passengers requiring wheelchair assistance. Ground staff has been informed.
Captain: Understood. The flight deck is fully prepared, and we are ready to commence boarding.
Purser: Copy that. We'll begin boarding as soon as the gate agent gives the go-ahead.
Captain: Please notify me once boarding is complete.
Purser: Will do, Captain.

Key Vocabulary

Term	Definition
boarding clearance	Final approval to begin passenger boarding
disarmed doors	Doors that are not yet armed with evacuation slides
emergency equipment	Safety tools such as fire extinguishers, oxygen bottles
wheelchair assistance	Service provided for passengers needing mobility support
galley secure	Galley area is checked and ready
go-ahead	Informal term for permission or clearance

Alternative Expressions

Original Expression	Alternative Expression
The cabin is ready.	The cabin is fully prepared.
Everything is in order.	All checks have been completed without issue.

We are ready to commence boarding.	We're good to go for boarding.
Ground staff has been informed.	The ground team is aware.
Please notify me once boarding is complete.	Let me know when boarding has finished.

Comprehension Check

Choose the correct answer or write a short response based on the dialogue.

1. What is the purpose of a safety check before boarding?

a) To verify catering services

b) To ensure equipment and procedures are in place for safe flight

c) To greet passengers with a smile

d) To record meal preferences

2. Who gives the final clearance to begin boarding?

a) Ground agent

b) Captain

c) Purser

d) First Officer

3. What safety step is confirmed as completed by the Purser?

a) Fueling the aircraft

b) Weather briefing

c) Cabin and security checks

d) Gate announcement

4. What phrase is used to confirm that checks have been completed?

5. What would you do if you found a missing piece of emergency equipment?

Role-play Activity Worksheet

Instructions:
Pair up and practice the following role-play situations using the vocabulary and expressions you learned in this unit. You may refer to the example dialogues as a guide. Try to be as natural and professional as possible.

Situation 1: Emergency Equipment Check
Role A (Senior Crew): Instruct your colleague to check the oxygen bottles and fire extinguisher.
Role B (Junior Crew): Respond with details of each item's status and confirm safety.

Objectives:
- Use proper reporting phrases.
- Mention pressure gauge, life vest seal, etc.

Situation 2: Cabin Seating Check
Role A: Ask your teammate to check seat belts, tray tables, and seat backs.
Role B: Walk through several seat rows and report your findings.

Objectives:
- Use action verbs (stowed, upright, fastened)
- Respond politely and clearly

• 항공운송 실무영어 Practical English for Cabin Crew

Wrap-up Quiz

Instructions:
Fill in the blanks or choose the correct option.

Part 1. Vocabulary Match
Match the word to its correct meaning.

Word	Definition
1. Galley	A. A small table in front of a passenger seat
2. Tray table	B. A device to put out a fire
3. Fire extinguisher	C. The aircraft's food preparation area
4. Seat back upright	D. The correct position for takeoff

Part 2: Fill in the blank
Complete each sentence with an appropriate word.

ready	disarmed
captain	wheelchair

5. The _____ gave final clearance to start boarding.

6. The Purser confirmed the cabin was _____ and all equipment was secure.

7. There were two passengers needing _____ assistance.

8. Cabin doors remain _____ until boarding is complete.

UNIT 03. Passenger Boarding & Greeting

Lesson objectives

By the end of this unit, students will be able to:
- Understand the importance of passenger boarding and greeting in cabin crew duties.
- Use appropriate English expressions for welcoming passengers and assisting during boarding.
- Demonstrate professional body language and tone when greeting passengers.
- Handle special boarding situations with confidence and courtesy.

Introduction

Passenger boarding is one of the most important phases of cabin crew duties, as it sets the tone for the entire flight. Greeting passengers at the aircraft door is more than a simple formality, it is a reflection of the airline's hospitality, professionalism, and commitment to service.

With a warm smile, polite greetings, and attentive body language, cabin crew create a welcoming atmosphere that helps passengers feel valued and reassured. This first interaction provides an opportunity to offer seat directions, assist passengers with special needs, and calm nervous travelers. A genuine and professional welcome not only leaves a positive first impression but also ensures a smooth boarding process, efficient passenger flow, and a strong representation of the airline's brand. By combining warmth, attentiveness, and efficiency, cabin crew lay the foundation for a safe, comfortable, and memorable flight experience.

Useful Expressions

Welcoming Passengers
- "Good morning! Welcome aboard."
- "Good afternoon! It's a pleasure to have you with us today."

- "Welcome aboard! May I help you find your seat?"

Offering Assistance

- "Please let me know if you need any help with your luggage."
- "Your seat is just down the aisle on the left."
- "If you need special assistance, I'll be happy to guide you."

Handling Special Situations

- Families with children: "Can I help you settle your child comfortably?"
- VIP passengers: "Welcome back, Mr./Ms. [Name]. We're glad to see you again."
- Late passengers: "Welcome aboard. Let me assist you to your seat quickly."

Warm-up 1

Label the boarding pass. Use the following words given.

	Words	Meaning in Korean
1		
2		
3		
4		
5		
6		
7		
8		

 Unit 03. Passenger Boarding & Greeting

Warm-up 2

Public Announcement on Ground for Cabin Crew Members

Purser :
Crew, standby for all interphone checks.
Crew, boarding clearance is given, passengers will be here shortly.
Crew, boarding position please.
As we are ready to depart, would all ground staff please disembark the aircraft for departure.
Cabin crew, Arm doors for departure and cross check.

Door operation
How to open and close door from inside and outside of the aircraft

Word & Phrases

Complete the sentences below using the words given in the view.

window seat	in the back
aisle	middle
boarding pass	go through
cabin	recheck
cooperation	step aside

1. Your seat is a _____.
2. Your seat is _____ of the cabin.
3. Please _____ the other aisle.
4. Thank you for your _____.
5. May I see your _____, please?
6. Your seat is in the _____ of the cabin.
7. You should keep this _____ open during boarding.
8. Would you please _____ to let other passengers through?
9. Your seat is in the next section of the _____.
10. We have to _____ the boarding pass for security reason.

· 항공운송 실무영어 Practical English for Cabin Crew

Warm-up 3

Complete the text by using these words in the box.

boarding pass	check-in
seating arrangements	overhead bins
seat number	in advance
window seats	hand-baggage (x2)

After 1 , passengers proceed to the aircraft with their 2 only. On arrival, they present their 3 , which has the 4 on it, to the cabin crew, who will show them where they should go. 5 are made at check-in. Many passengers prefer 6

to aisle seats and often insist on booking them 7 . Passengers can ask for help to put their 8 into the 9 .

1.   4.   7.
2.   5.   8.
3.   6.   9.

Practical Knowledge

Seat configuration

Seat configuration refers to the arrangement of seats in an aircraft, usually indicating the number of seats in each row and how they are divided by aisles. It is often represented as a combination of numbers and letters (e.g., 3-3, 2-4-2, 3-3-3) that describes how seats are grouped together in different sections of the cabin.

- **Narrow-body planes (single aisle)**: Common configurations are 3-3 or 2-2.
- **Wide-body planes (two aisles)**: Common configurations include 3-3-3 or 2-4-2)

Unit 03. Passenger Boarding & Greeting

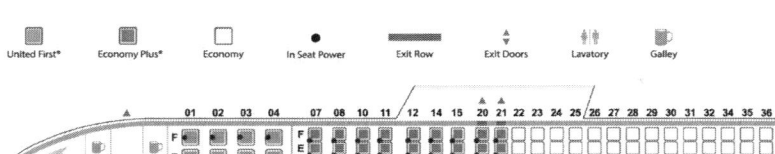

Boeing 737-800 Seat Map

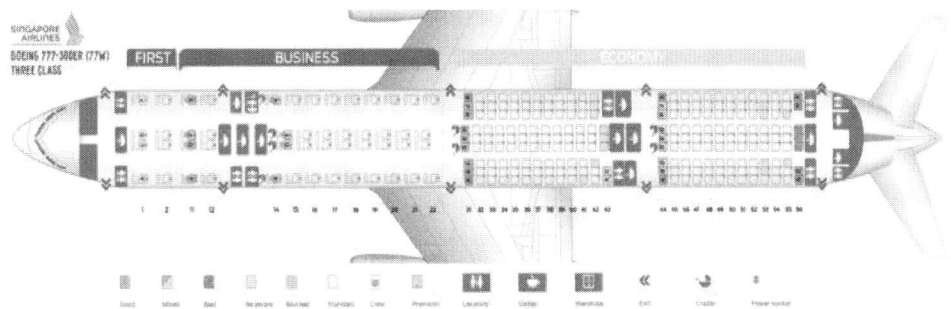

Boeing 777-300ER Seat Map

• 항공운송 실무영어 Practical English for Cabin Crew

Speaking Practice

Practice speaking English by making different sentences using the phrases below.

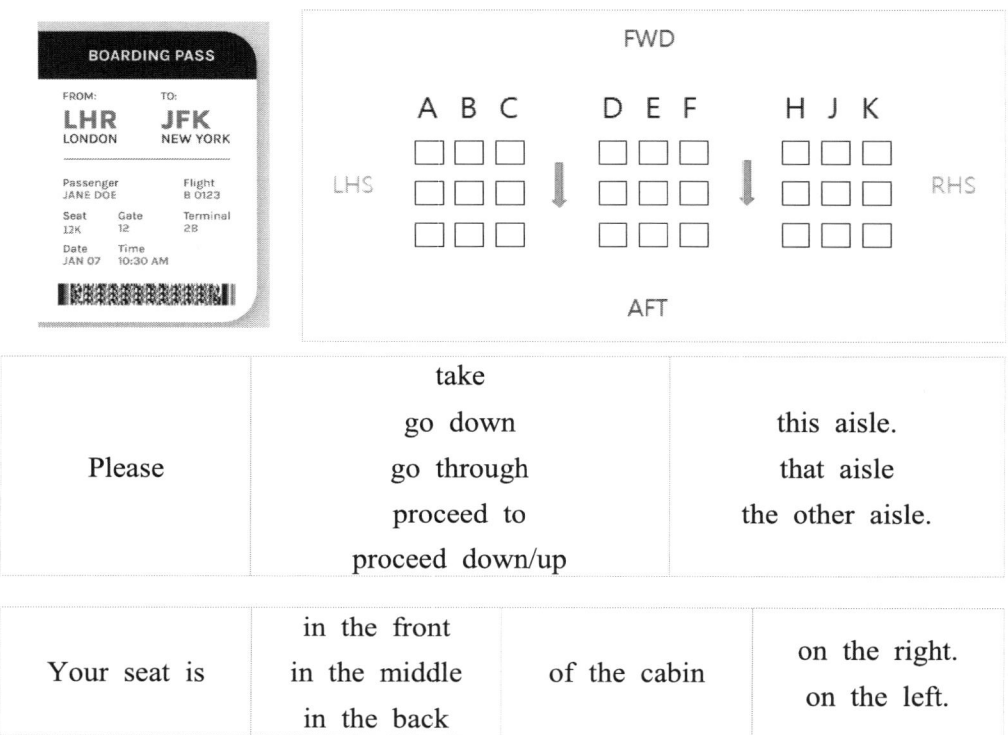

Please	take go down go through proceed to proceed down/up		this aisle. that aisle the other aisle.
Your seat is	in the front in the middle in the back	of the cabin	on the right. on the left.

 Unit 03. Passenger Boarding & Greeting

Conversations

Situation 1: Welcoming and greeting passengers at the door

Setting:
At the aircraft entrance during the initial stage of boarding. A cabin crew member is greeting passengers and checking their boarding passes while guiding them to their assigned seats.

Characters:
- Cabin Crew
- Purser

Dialogue

Cabin Crew: Good morning. Welcome aboard. May I see your boarding pass, please?
Passenger: Hello. Here it is.
Cabin Crew: Thank you. Please take this way. Your seat is in the front of the cabin, on your right. It's a window seat.
Passenger: Thank you.
Cabin Crew: You're welcome. Have a good flight.

Key Vocabulary

Vocabulary	Meaning
initial	happening at the beginning; first
boarding pass	A document or digital ticket that shows your flight and seat details.
assigned	given to someone as a duty, task, or responsibility; designated
guiding	leading or showing the way; giving direction or advice
cabin	The main area inside the aircraft where passengers are seated.
window seat	A passenger seat next to the window.

· 항공운송 실무영어 Practical English for Cabin Crew

Alternative Expressions

Original Expression	Alternative Expression
Good morning. Welcome aboard.	Hello. Nice to have you with us.
May I see your boarding pass, please?	Could I check your boarding pass?
Please take this way.	This way, please. / You can follow me this way.
Your seat is in the front of the cabin.	Your seat is located toward the front of the aircraft.
Have a good flight.	Enjoy your flight. / Wish you a pleasant journey.

Situation 2: Assisting a Passenger Who Refuses to Show a Boarding Pass

Setting:
At the aircraft entrance during boarding. The cabin crew is checking each passenger's boarding pass to confirm seating and ensure safety procedures. A passenger insists he knows his seat and initially refuses to show the pass.

Characters:
- Cabin Crew
- Passenger

Dialogue

Cabin Crew: Good afternoon, sir. Welcome aboard. Let me check your boarding pass.

Passenger: I know where to sit. My seat is 35E.

Cabin Crew: I'm sorry, sir, but we have to recheck the boarding pass for security reasons.

Passenger: Oh, I see. Here you are.

Cabin Crew: Thank you for your cooperation. Please keep going down this aisle. Your seat is a middle seat on your left.

Unit 03. Passenger Boarding & Greeting

Key Vocabulary

Vocabulary	Meaning
recheck	To check something again for confirmation.
cooperation	The act of working together or complying politely.
aisle	A walkway between seats on an airplane.
middle seat	The seat located between the window and aisle seats.
security reasons	Rules or policies related to passenger and flight safety.

Alternative Expressions

Original Expression	Alternative Expression
Good afternoon, sir. Welcome aboard.	Hello, welcome on board, sir.
Let me check your boarding pass.	May I see your boarding pass, please?
I know where to sit.	I already know my seat.
We have to recheck the boarding pass for security reason.	We need to double-check it for security purposes.
Thank you for cooperation.	I appreciate your understanding.
Please keep going down this aisle.	Please continue straight down this path.
Your seat is a middle seat on your left.	You'll find your seat in the middle, to your left.

Situation 3: Assisting Passengers to Find Their Seat

Setting:
Inside the aircraft cabin during active boarding. A passenger is having trouble locating their assigned seat and seeks assistance from a nearby cabin crew member. The crew member responds with clear, professional guidance.

Characters:
- Cabin Crew
- Passenger

Dialogue

Passenger: Excuse me, I can't seem to find my seat.
Cabin Crew: Let me help you. May I see your boarding pass, please?
Passenger: Here it is.
Cabin Crew: Thank you. You're in seat 12A. It's just down this aisle on the left-hand side.
Passenger: Thank you so much.
Cabin Crew: You're welcome. Please let me know if you need anything else.

Key Vocabulary

Vocabulary	Meaning
Left-hand side	The side to the left when facing forward.
Seat number	The assigned number/letter combination for a passenger's seat.
Assigned seat	The specific seat designated to a passenger.

Alternative Expressions

Original Expression	Alternative Expression
I can't seem to find my seat.	I'm having trouble locating my seat.
Let me help you.	I'll assist you with that.
May I see your boarding pass, please?	Could you show me your boarding pass?
You're in seat 12A.	Your seat is 12A.
It's just down this aisle on the left-hand side.	Walk down this aisle, and it's on your left.
Please let me know if you need anything else.	Feel free to ask if you need further assistance.

Unit 03. Passenger Boarding & Greeting

Wrap-up Quiz

Part 1. Fill in the blanks

Instructions:

Fill in the blanks using the correct words from the box below. (Some words may not be used.)

boarding pass	window seat
aisle	left-hand side
cabin	life vest
cooperation	security
boarding	galley

1. May I see your _____, please?
2. Your seat is on the _____ of the cabin, next to the window.
3. Please walk down this _____ and turn right at Row 12.
4. Thank you for your _____. Enjoy your flight!
5. The _____ was prepared before passengers started boarding.

Part 2. Put the Sentences in Order

Instructions:

The following sentences describe a typical boarding interaction between a cabin crew member and a passenger. Rearrange them into the correct order (1-5).

Sentences (Random Order):

A. "You're in seat 21B. Please continue straight down this aisle and it will be on your right."
B. "Good afternoon. Welcome aboard!"
C. "Here's my boarding pass."
D. "May I see your boarding pass, please?"
E. "Thank you. Enjoy your flight!"

항공운송 실무영어 Practical English for Cabin Crew

Role-play Activity Worksheet

Instructions:
1. Work in pairs. One person plays the role of the Cabin Crew, and the other plays the Passenger.
2. Use the target vocabulary and expressions from the dialogue.
3. After practicing, switch roles and try again with different seat numbers or locations.

Role-play Scenarios

Scenario 1

A passenger is confused and cannot find seat 7C. Help guide them to the correct seat.
- Cabin Crew: Greet the passenger, check the boarding pass, and explain the seat location.
- Passenger: Politely ask for help and respond to directions.

Scenario 2

A passenger is seated in the wrong seat. Assist in checking their boarding pass and directing them properly.
- Cabin Crew: Point out the mistake gently, help the passenger find the correct seat.
- Passenger: Respond with understanding and follow directions.

Scenario 3 (Advanced)

A family is seated apart due to last-minute changes. Try to find a solution or offer alternatives.
- Cabin Crew: Apologize, check the seat map, offer to ask other passengers if a switch is possible.
- Passenger: Express concern and respond with flexibility or appreciation.

Unit 04. Handling Carry-on Baggage and Special Handling Passengers

UNIT 04. Handling Carry-on Baggage and Special Handling Passengers

Learning Objectives

By the end of this unit, students will be able to:
- Identify and respond to common seating issues during passenger boarding.
- Use polite and effective English expressions when resolving seat-related problems.
- Assist with seat changes due to mistakes, preferences, or special needs.
- Practice clear and professional communication when coordinating seat swaps.

Introduction

Seating issues are common challenges that cabin crew encounter during the boarding process. Passengers may sit in the wrong seat, request to change seats, or need special accommodations due to physical conditions or travel companions. Cabin crew must handle these situations professionally and efficiently, while maintaining a positive and calm attitude.

In this unit, you will learn how to assist passengers with seating problems and requests using polite and clear English. You will also practice how to negotiate seat swaps with other passengers and respond to requests for aisle, window, or extra legroom seats.

Boarding and Seating
- Passengers with infants are often allowed to board early, providing extra time to settle into their seats.

Stroller Policy
- Strollers can typically be used until the passenger reaches the boarding gate. At that point, they are tagged and stored in the cargo hold.

- Upon arrival, the stroller will either be returned at the aircraft door or at the baggage claim area, depending on the airport policy.

Infant Safety
- For safety during takeoff, landing, and turbulence, passengers are provided with an infant seatbelt that must be properly secured.

Amenities and Assistance
- Airlines often provide amenities for infants, such as baby food, milk, and diapers. Let the passenger know they can request these items from the cabin crew.
- Cabin crew can assist with tasks such as warming bottles or providing additional blankets for the infant.

Emergency Information
- In case of an emergency, passengers should always secure their own oxygen mask first before assisting their infant.

Briefing of a passenger travelling with an infant

Unit 04. Handling Carry-on Baggage and Special Handling Passengers

Practical Knowledge

At the Gate
- **Stroller Drop-Off:**
  - The stroller is typically left at the aircraft door or handed over to ground staff for cargo storage.
  - Confirm with the passenger where and when they will receive the stroller (usually at the destination gate or baggage claim).
- **Assist with Carrying Baby or Luggage:**
  - Offer assistance to the passenger in carrying the baby or handling their carry-on bags.

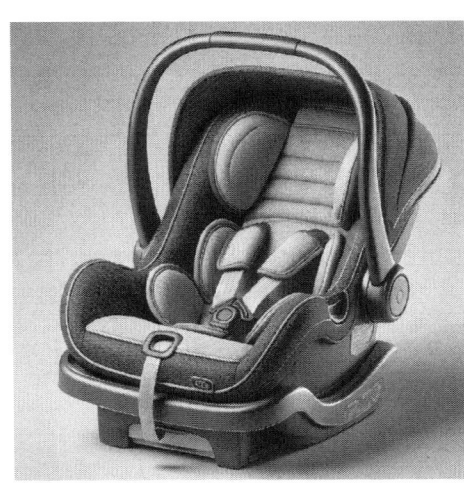

At the Gate
- **Carrier Check or Use Confirmation:**
  - If the car seat carrier is to be checked instead of used on the aircraft, ensure it is tagged appropriately and stored in the cargo hold.
  - If the car seat is to be used on board, confirm the seat assignment (typically a window seat for safety reasons).
- **Pre-Boarding Assistance:**
  - Offer assistance in carrying the car seat carrier, luggage, or infant if the passenger requires help.

• 항공운송 실무영어 Practical English for Cabin Crew

Key Vocabulary

Word / Phrase	Meaning
wrong seat	A seat that is not the one assigned to the passenger
seat assignment	The specific seat number given to a passenger
aisle seat	A seat next to the aisle
window seat	A seat next to the window
middle seat	The seat between the aisle and window seats
seat swap	An exchange of seats between passengers
bulkhead seat	A seat located behind a partition wall, often with extra legroom
exit row	A row of seats next to the emergency exit, often with more space
special request	A specific seating preference or need (e.g. sitting with family)
comply	To follow or agree with a request or rule
accommodate	To meet someone's needs or requests
overbooked	When more passengers are booked than there are seats available

Useful Expressions

Situation	Example Expression
Asking to check a passenger's seat	May I see your boarding pass, please?
Informing of a seating error	I'm sorry, but you are in the wrong seat.
Guiding to the correct seat	Your seat is in row 16, on the left side by the window.
Offering to help with a swap	Would you be willing to change seats so this family can sit together?
Responding to a seating request	Let me see what I can do for you.
Asking another passenger for a favor	Excuse me, would you mind switching seats with this passenger?
Handling refusal to swap seats	I understand. Thank you for your consideration.
Confirming resolution	Thank you for your cooperation.

Unit 04. Handling Carry-on Baggage and Special Handling Passengers

Conversations

Situation 1: Wrong Seat

Setting:
During boarding, a cabin crew member finds a passenger sitting in the wrong seat.

Characters:
- Cabin Crew
- Passenger

Dialogue

Cabin Crew: Good afternoon, ma'am. May I check your boarding pass?
Passenger: Sure, here you go.
Cabin Crew: Thank you. I see that your assigned seat is 18C, but this is 18A.
Passenger: Oh, really? I must have read it wrong.
Cabin Crew: No problem. Let me help you find your correct seat. Please follow me this way.
Passenger: Thank you. Sorry about the confusion.
Cabin Crew: It's absolutely fine. Please let me know if you need anything else.

Key Vocabulary

Vocabulary	Meaning
boarding pass	a document that shows your assigned seat and allows you to board the aircraft
aisle	the walkway between rows of seats
misread	to read something incorrectly
across	on the opposite side of something

Alternative Expressions

Original Expression	Alternative Expression
May I check your boarding pass?	Could I take a look at your boarding pass?

• 항공운송 실무영어 Practical English for Cabin Crew

It seems your seat is...	According to your boarding pass, your seat is...
No problem at all.	That's okay.

Situation 2: Seat Swap Request

Setting:
A passenger requests to switch seats with another for personal reasons, and the cabin crew mediates politely.

Characters:
- Cabin Crew
- Passenger A (wants to change seat)
- Passenger B (has the requested seat)

Dialogue

Passenger A: Excuse me, is it possible to switch my seat?
Cabin Crew: May I ask why you'd like to change your seat?
Passenger A: I'd like to sit next to my friend. She's in 14A and I'm in 17C.
Cabin Crew: Let me check with the passenger in 14B.
Passenger B: I don't mind switching.
Cabin Crew: Thank you very much. Passenger A, please take your new seat.

Key Vocabulary & Phrases

Vocabulary	Meaning
switch seats	to exchange seats with someone
next to	beside or adjacent to someone
passenger	someone traveling in a vehicle, especially a plane

Alternative Expressions

Original Expression	Alternative Expression
Is it possible to switch my seat?	Is it okay to change my seat? Can I take another seat, if it's available? Could I change my seat, please?

Unit 04. Handling Carry-on Baggage and Special Handling Passengers

Let me check with the passenger.	I'll ask the other passenger. I'll see if the passenger is okay with it. Let me speak with the passenger first.
I don't mind switching.	It's fine with me. I'm okay with changing seats. No problem, I can change.

Situation 3: Traveling with an Infant and a Stroller

Setting:
At the aircraft door during passenger boarding. A passenger carrying an infant and a stroller approaches the cabin crew for assistance.

Characters:
- Cabin Crew
- Passenger

Dialogue

Cabin Crew: Good afternoon! Welcome aboard [Airline Name]. May I assist you today?
Purser: Hello, thank you. I'm traveling with my baby and a stroller. What should I do with the stroller?
Cabin Crew: No problem. You can fold the stroller, and our ground staff will store it in the cargo hold. You'll receive it back at the arrival gate.
Purser: That's great. Could I keep my baby's car seat on board?
Cabin Crew: Yes, if it is an approved child safety seat, you may use it in your assigned seat. Let me help you check.
Purser: Thank you so much. Boarding with a baby can be stressful.
Cabin Crew: You're doing just fine. Please follow me, and I'll guide you to your seat. If you need any assistance during the flight, don't hesitate to let us know.
Purser: I appreciate your help.

Key Vocabulary

Word/Phrase	Meaning
infant	a baby or very young child.

• 항공운송 실무영어 Practical English for Cabin Crew

stroller	a small carriage with wheels used to carry a baby.
fold (a stroller)	to collapse a stroller so it can be stored easily.
cargo hold	the storage area of the aircraft beneath the passenger cabin.
car seat	a special seat designed for safely securing an infant on board.
assigned seat	the passenger's designated place on the aircraft.

Alternative Expressions

Original Expression	Alternative Expression
May I assist you today?	Do you need any help with your baby or stroller?
You'll receive it back at the arrival gate.	The stroller will be returned to you right after landing.
Please follow me, and I'll guide you to your seat.	Let me show you the way to your seat.

Situation 4: Request for Special Seat (Aisle/Window)

Setting:
A passenger requests to switch seats with another for personal reasons, and the cabin crew mediates politely.

Characters:
- Cabin Crew
- Passenger

Dialogue

Passenger A: Excuse me, is it possible to switch my seat?
Cabin Crew: May I ask why you'd like to change your seat?
Passenger A: I'd like to sit next to my friend. She's in 14A and I'm in 17C.
Cabin Crew: Let me check with the passenger in 14B.
Passenger B: I don't mind switching.
Cabin Crew: Thank you very much. Passenger A, please take your new seat.

Unit 04. Handling Carry-on Baggage and Special Handling Passengers

Key Vocabulary

Vocabulary	Meaning
aisle seat	a seat next to the aisle
stretch	to extend your limbs or body
available	free to use or not occupied
in luck	fortunate; having good luck

Alternative Expressions

Original Expression	Alternative Expression
Is there any chance...?	Would it be possible...?
Let me check ~	I'll see if ~
You're in luck.	Fortunately, we have one.

Situation 5: Duplicate Seat Assignment

Setting:
Two passengers present the same seat number on their boarding passes. The cabin crew handles the situation calmly and checks the manifest.

Characters:
- Cabin Crew
- Passenger A
- Passenger B

Dialogue

Passenger A: Excuse me, someone is already in my seat.
Cabin Crew: Let me take a look at both your boarding passes.
Passenger B: Mine also says 23D.
Cabin Crew: Thank you. It seems there's been a duplicate seat assignment. I'll verify with the gate agent.
Cabin Crew (after checking): Passenger A, you've been reassigned to 24F. I'll help you settle in.
Passenger A: Thank you for resolving this quickly.

· 항공운송 실무영어 Practical English for Cabin Crew

Key Vocabulary

Vocabulary	Meaning
duplicate	a copy or something that appears more than once
verify	to check or confirm
reassigned	given a new position or seat
resolve	to fix a problem

Alternative Expressions

Original Expression	Alternative Expression
Let me take a look at...	May I check...?
I'll verify with the gate agent.	I'll contact the ground staff.
You've been reassigned.	Your seat has been changed.

Situation 6: Assisting a Wheelchair Passenger during Boarding

Setting:
During pre-boarding, a cabin crew member greets a passenger in a wheelchair being escorted onto the aircraft. The crew ensures the passenger's comfort, provides safety-related assistance, and coordinates seat access and storage needs.

Characters:
- Cabin Crew
- Wheelchair Passenger
- Ground Staff

Dialogue

Cabin Crew: Good morning. Welcome aboard. May I assist you to your seat?
Passenger: Yes, please. I'd appreciate some help transferring to the seat.
Cabin Crew: Of course. May I check your seat number?
Passenger: I'm in 7D. It's an aisle seat, I believe.
Cabin Crew: Yes, that's right. It's just here on your left. I'll help you get settled in.
Passenger: Thank you so much. Could you store my small bag?
Cabin Crew: Absolutely. I'll place it in the overhead bin and keep it easily

Unit 04. Handling Carry-on Baggage and Special Handling Passengers

accessible. Would you like me to bring it to you during the flight if needed?
Passenger: That would be great.
Cabin Crew: Once you're seated, I'll go over the nearest emergency exits and safety features. Let me know if you have any specific needs or concerns.
Passenger: Thanks. I feel more at ease now.
Cabin Crew: I'm glad to hear that. We're here to make your journey as safe and comfortable as possible.

Key Vocabulary

Word / Phrase	Meaning
transfer (to seat)	Moving from the wheelchair to the aircraft seat
accessible seat	A seat designated or suitable for passengers with mobility needs
overhead bin	Storage area above passenger seats
aisle seat	A seat next to the aisle or walkway between seat rows
emergency exit	A designated door for emergency evacuation
settle in	To become comfortably seated
special assistance	Support given to passengers with specific physical needs
escort	A person accompanying or helping the passenger
safety briefing	Explanation of how to stay safe during the flight

Alternative Expressions

Original Expression	Alternative Expression
May I assist you to your seat?	Can I help you get to your seat? Would you like help boarding?
I'll help you get settled in.	Let me help you get comfortable. I'll make sure you're seated safely.
I'll place it in the overhead bin.	I'll store your bag above for you.
Let me know if you have any concerns.	Please feel free to speak up if you need anything.
We're here to make your journey comfortable.	Our goal is to ensure your comfort and safety.

• 항공운송 실무영어 Practical English for Cabin Crew

Comprehension Check

Check your understanding of the dialogues. Choose the correct answer.

1. What did the cabin crew do when a passenger sat in the wrong seat?

a) Asked the passenger to leave

b) Checked the boarding pass and guided them to the correct seat

c) Called the captain

d) Ignored the mistake

2. Why did a passenger request a seat change?

a) They wanted a window seat

b) They were afraid of flying

c) They wanted to sit next to a friend

d) They had a food allergy

3. How did the crew respond to a duplicate seat assignment?

a) Asked both passengers to stand

b) Assigned one passenger to a jump seat

c) Contacted the gate agent and reassigned a seat

d) Ignored the issue

4. What was the reason the passenger requested an aisle seat?

a) They wanted to look out the window

b) They had a leg condition

c) They were traveling with a baby

d) They didn't like the middle seat

5. What is the crew's attitude when assisting with seating problems?

a) Impatient and strict.

b) Formal and passive

c) Friendly and solution-oriented

d) Unconcerned

Unit 04. Handling Carry-on Baggage and Special Handling Passengers

Wrap-up Quiz

Complete the sentences using the correct words from the list below.

boarding pass	switch
aisle	condition
duplicate	across
assist	assigned
verify	seat map

1. The flight attendant asked the passenger to show their _____.

2. The cabin crew offered to _____ a passenger with a seating problem.

3. A _____ seat number was printed on two passengers' tickets.

4. The cabin crew had to _____ the correct seating from the manifest.

5. The passenger requested to _____ seats with someone next to their friend.

6. A medical _____ required the passenger to request an aisle seat.

7. The seat was located _____ the aisle, on the right side.

8. Each passenger was _____ a specific seat based on the ticket.

9. The _____ helped the cabin crew locate available spots.

10. The flight attendant walked down the _____ to help the passengers.

・항공운송 실무영어 Practical English for Cabin Crew

Role-play Activity Worksheet

Practice the real-life situations with your partner. Use polite and professional English.

Instructions:
- Work in pairs (A & B)
- Each pair will perform 2 role-play situations
- Use the sample dialogue as a guide, but personalize your responses
- Focus on tone, vocabulary, and non-verbal communication (e.g. smile, eye contact)

Role-play 1: Passenger Sitting in the Wrong Seat
- Student A: Cabin Crew
- Student B: Passenger who mistakenly sat in 12C instead of 14A
- Goal: Politely inform the passenger and help them relocate

Role-play 2: Request to Change Seats
- Student A: Passenger wanting to sit next to a friend
- Student B: Cabin Crew
- Goal: Explain the request and check if seat swap is possible

Role-play 3: Special Seat Request
- Student A: Passenger with medical needs requesting an aisle seat
- Student B: Cabin Crew
- Goal: Ask for the reason and offer available alternatives

Role-play 4: Duplicate Seat Assignment
- Student A & B: Passengers with same seat number
- Student C: Cabin Crew
- Goal: Calmly resolve the issue by verifying information

Unit05. Pre-Departure Announcements & Checks

UNIT 05. Pre-Departure Announcements & Checks

Learning Objectives

By the end of this unit, learners will be able to:
- Deliver and understand key announcements made before takeoff.
- Use clear and polite English when performing final cabin checks.
- Communicate safety-related instructions and respond to passenger needs.

Introduction

Before departure, cabin crew are responsible for delivering important announcements and performing a series of final safety and service checks. This phase is crucial in preparing both passengers and crew for a safe takeoff. Announcements may include greetings, safety demonstration guidance, electronic device regulations, and reminders for seatbelt fastening and tray table storage. Simultaneously, crew members move through the cabin to verify compliance and assist passengers as needed.

Tasks include:
- Delivering safety announcements (via interphone or manually)
- Monitoring passenger compliance (seatbelt, tray tables, window shades)
- Checking lavatories and galleys
- Arming doors and completing cross-check
- Reporting readiness to the purser or flight deck

Safety Demonstration

A safety demonstration is the briefing given by cabin crew before take-off to ensure that all passengers are familiar with the safety equipment and emergency procedures of the aircraft. It is a legal requirement in commercial aviation and must be completed on every flight.

The purpose of the safety demonstration is to increase passenger awareness and prepare them for unexpected situations, such as emergency landings, cabin depressurization, or evacuation.

Key Elements of a Safety Demonstration:
1. **Seat Belts** - How to fasten, adjust, and unfasten the seatbelt.
2. **Oxygen Masks** - How to properly use the oxygen mask in case of sudden cabin depressurization.
3. **Life Vests** - Where the life vest is located and how to wear and inflate it.
4. **Emergency Exits** - The location of all exits and how to operate them.
5. **Safety Cards** - Encouragement to read the safety information card in the seat pocket.
6. **Electronic Devices** - Rules regarding the use of mobile phones and electronic devices during the flight.

Types of Demonstrations:
- Live Demonstration: Performed directly by the cabin crew in the aisle.
- Video Demonstration: Shown on overhead screens or personal monitors.
- Hybrid: A video is played, and crew members supplement with gestures or additional explanations.

Importance:
- Helps passengers know what to do in an emergency.
- Ensures that even frequent travelers are reminded of safety rules.
- Reduces panic and confusion during unexpected situations.

Safety Demonstration Video

Safety Video

A safety video is a pre-recorded instructional film shown to passengers before take-off. It delivers the same information as a live safety demonstration by the cabin crew, but in a standardized and visually engaging format.

Unit 05. Pre-Departure Announcements & Checks

Purpose of a Safety Video
- To inform passengers about essential safety procedures on board.
- To ensure consistency across all flights, regardless of crew or aircraft type.
- To capture attention through visual aids, animations, or cultural/creative elements.

Common Contents of a Safety Video
1. Seat Belt Instructions – How to fasten, tighten, and release.
2. Oxygen Mask Usage – Steps to follow during cabin depressurization.
3. Life Vest Demonstration – How to wear and inflate the vest.
4. Emergency Exits – Showing all exit doors and escape paths.
5. Safety Card Reminder – Encouraging passengers to review the safety card.
6. No Smoking & Electronic Devices – Explaining prohibited items and device usage.

Features of Modern Safety Videos
- Cultural themes: Airlines often include cultural references (e.g. Korean Air showing Korean traditions).
- Entertainment value: Some airlines use humor, celebrities, or animation (e.g. Air New Zealand's "Hobbit" themed safety video).
- Multilingual support: Subtitles or narration in multiple languages to reach all passengers.

Safety Video-Turkish Airlines

Safety Video-Korean Air

Practical Knowledge

1. Arming the door
- **Purpose**: This ensures the evacuation slide is ready for use in case of an emergency evacuation.
- **Procedure**: Typically performed after all passengers have boarded and before the aircraft leaves the gate. The cabin crew engages the door lever or switch that "arms" the slide mechanism.

2. Disarming the door
- **Purpose**: This is done during normal operations when the aircraft has landed and is at the gate, allowing passengers to safely deplane without accidentally deploying the slide.
- **Procedure**: Performed by the cabin crew before the door is opened, usually after the aircraft has come to a complete stop and the parking brake is set.

Conversations

Situation 1: Making a Welcome and Safety Announcement

Setting:
The cabin crew is preparing for departure. The purser makes the welcome and safety announcement over the PA system while other crew members prepare for the safety demonstration.

Characters:
- Purser
- Cabin crew
- Passengers (in background)

Public Announcement

Purser:
"Ladies and gentlemen, welcome onboard Flight KE131 bound for Los Angeles.
We are pleased to have you with us today. Please place all carry-on items in the overhead compartment or under the seat in front of you, and take your seats as we prepare for departure."

Unit 05. Pre-Departure Announcements & Checks

Purser:
"For your safety, please fasten your seatbelt, ensure your seat back is in the upright position, and your tray table is securely stowed."

Purser:
"We would like to remind you that all electronic devices must now be turned off or set to airplane mode. Smoking is strictly prohibited on this aircraft, including in the lavatories."

Purser:
"We will now demonstrate the safety features of this aircraft. Even if you are a frequent flyer, we ask that you give us your full attention. Thank you."
Soojin and Jae (Cabin Crew):
(Begin safety demonstration in the aisle using gestures and equipment)

Key Vocabulary & Phrases

Term / Phrase	Meaning
welcome onboard	greeting passengers onto the plane
bound for [destination]	going to a specific destination
carry-on item	small personal luggage brought into the cabin
overhead compartment	storage space above passenger seats
seat back in the upright position	seat is fully vertical for safety
tray table securely stowed	tray folded and locked in place
airplane mode	mobile device setting disabling signal transmission
lavatory	aircraft restroom
safety demonstration	explanation of emergency procedures
frequent flyer	someone who travels by air regularly

· 항공운송 실무영어 Practical English for Cabin Crew

Alternative Expressions

Original Expression	Alternative Expression
Welcome onboard.	We're delighted to have you with us.
Flight bound for Los Angeles.	Our destination today is Los Angeles.
Please fasten your seatbelt.	Kindly secure your seatbelt low and tight across your lap.
Your tray table is securely stowed.	Please make sure your tray is folded and locked.
Give us your full attention.	We appreciate your attention during this important demonstration.

Situation 2: Politely Asking a Passenger to Fasten Seatbelt and Prepare for Takeoff

Setting:
Cabin crew is conducting the final cabin check before departure. One passenger has not fastened their seatbelt and still has their seat reclined.

Characters:
- Cabin Crew
- Passenger

Dialogue

Cabin Crew:
Excuse me, sir. May I ask you to fasten your seatbelt, please?

Passenger:
Oh, I didn't realize it was unfastened. Sorry about that.

Cabin Crew:
No problem at all. And if you could also return your seat to the upright position, that would be great.

Passenger:
Sure. Is this okay now?

Unit 05. Pre-Departure Announcements & Checks

Cabin Crew:
Yes, thank you. Lastly, please stow your tray table and make sure your bag is placed completely under the seat in front of you.

Passenger:
Got it. Thanks for letting me know.

Cabin Crew:
You're welcome. We'll be taking off shortly. Enjoy your flight.

Key Vocabulary & Phrases

Term / Phrase	Meaning
fasten your seatbelt	secure the seatbelt around your waist
return your seat to the upright position	move the seatback to a vertical angle
stow	store or place properly
tray table	small table attached to the seatback
under the seat in front of you	the space for storing bags during takeoff/landing
no problem at all	polite response to an apology
enjoy your flight	a courteous farewell before takeoff

Alternative Expressions

Original Expression	Alternative Expression
Fasten your seatbelt.	Please make sure your seatbelt is securely buckled.
Return your seat to the upright position.	Could you bring your seat back up, please?
Stow your tray table.	Please fold and lock your tray table.
Make sure your bag is under the seat.	Kindly place your bag fully under the seat in front.
Enjoy your flight.	Have a pleasant journey.

・항공운송 실무영어 Practical English for Cabin Crew

Situation 3: Arming Doors and Reporting Readiness

Setting:
All passengers are seated and the final checks are complete. The purser gives the command to arm the doors. Cabin crew follow procedures and report back.

Characters:
- Purser
- Cabin Crew (2L)
- Cabin Crew (2R)

Dialogue

Purser:
Cabin crew, arm all doors and cross-check.

Cabin Crew (2L):
L2 door armed and cross-checked.

Cabin Crew (2R):
R2 door armed and cross-checked.

Purser:
Thank you. I will now inform the flight deck that the cabin is secure and we are ready for departure.

Key Vocabulary

Term / Phrase	Meaning
arm the door	activate the emergency evacuation slide mechanism
cross-check	verify procedures with another crew member
L2 / R2 door	left/right side second door on the aircraft
cabin is secure	all safety checks are completed
inform the flight deck	notify the pilots (captain/first officer)

Unit 05. Pre-Departure Announcements & Checks

Alternative Expressions

Original Expression	Alternative Expression
Cabin crew, arm all doors and cross-check	Set doors to armed mode and verify with team
2L door armed and cross-checked	2L door set for emergency use, status confirmed
Cross-check complete	Door verification complete
Cabin is secure	All safety checks have been completed
Inform the flight deck	Notify the cockpit that the cabin is ready

Situation 4: Reporting a Cabin Irregularity

Setting:
A cabin crew member notices a suspicious item in a seat pocket during the final cabin check. The crew member reports the issue to the purser before takeoff.

Characters:
Cabin Crew
Purser

Dialogue

Cabin Crew:
Purser, I found a suspicious-looking battery pack in the seat pocket at 21C. It doesn't have a label and looks damaged.

Purser:
Thank you. Please place it in the cabin safety bag immediately and inform the flight deck.

• 항공운송 실무영어 Practical English for Cabin Crew

Cabin Crew:
Understood. I'll also make a note in the cabin log.

Purser:
Good. Please continue with your checks after securing the item.

Cabin Crew: Will do.

Key Vocabulary

Term / Phrase	Meaning
suspicious item	Object that appears unsafe or unusual
battery pack	Portable charging device
seat pocket	Storage space behind a passenger seat
cabin safety bag	Bag used to store hazardous items
flight deck	Cockpit; where pilots are seated
make a note	Record the situation in the official log

Alternative Expressions

Original Expression	Alternative Expression
I found a suspicious-looking battery pack	There's an unusual battery pack I discovered
It doesn't have a label	It appears to be unmarked
Place it in the cabin safety bag	Store it safely in the designated safety pouch
Inform the flight deck	Notify the captain about the situation
I'll make a note in the cabin log	I'll record this incident in the flight log

Unit 05. Pre-Departure Announcements & Checks

Situation 5: Reporting "Cabin is Ready" to the Captain

Setting:
Cabin checks and door arming are complete. The purser contacts the flight deck via interphone to report that the cabin is secure and ready for takeoff.

Characters:
- Purser
- Flight Deck (Captain or First Officer)

Dialogue

Purser (over interphone):
Flight deck, this is the cabin. All doors are armed and cross-checked. Final cabin check is complete.

Flight Deck:
Copy that. Is the cabin secure for departure?

Purser:
Affirmative. Cabin is secure and ready for takeoff.

Flight Deck:
Thank you. We'll be pushing back shortly.

Purser:
Understood. Standing by for further instructions.

Key Vocabulary

Term / Phrase	Meaning
cabin is secure	All safety checks are complete, and the cabin is ready
pushback	Aircraft being moved away from the gate
standing by	Waiting and ready for the next instruction
cross-checked	Safety procedures verified with another crew
affirmative	Formal way to say "yes" or "confirmed"

• 항공운송 실무영어 Practical English for Cabin Crew

Alternative Expressions

Original Expression	Alternative Expression
Final cabin check is complete	Cabin safety inspection has been finished
Cabin is secure and ready for takeoff	All checks are complete. We are ready for departure
Copy that	Received and understood
Standing by for further instructions	Awaiting your next command
All doors are armed and cross-checked	Emergency exits are set and verified

Wrap-Up Quiz

Part 1: Fill in the Blank - Use the Words in the Box

| seatbelt | upright | stow | demonstration | cross-check |

1. Please return your seat to the _____ position.
   → _____

2. Cabin crew, arm all doors and _____.
   → _____

3. We will now begin the safety _____ of this aircraft.
   → _____

4. Kindly _____ your bag in the overhead bin or under the seat.
   → _____

5. All passengers must fasten their _____ before takeoff.
   → _____

Unit 05. Pre-Departure Announcements & Checks

Part 2: Match the Expression with the Meaning

Expression	Meaning
6. Fasten your seatbelt	A. Return the seat to a vertical position
7. Stow your belongings	B. Buckle the belt across your lap
8. Seatback upright	C. Store items in the correct place
9. Safety demonstration	D. Show how to use emergency equipment

Part 3: True or False - Circle T (True) or F (False)

Statement	T / F
10. Cabin crew can delay arming doors until after takeoff.	T / F
11. The purser contacts the flight deck once the cabin is secure.	T / F
12. Tray tables can remain open during takeoff as long as they are empty.	T / F
13. "Cross-check" means verifying that safety procedures are complete.	T / F

14. What does "arm the doors" mean?

a) Open the aircraft doors for boarding

b) Activate the emergency slide system

c) Lock the cabin door from outside

d) Set the door to maintenance mode

15. What does a cabin crew member check during the final cabin check?

a) Passenger meal preferences

b) Tray tables, seatbelts, overhead bins

c) Weather at the destination

d) Pilot communication system

16. What should passengers do with electronic devices before takeoff?
a) Use freely
b) Set to airplane mode or turn off
c) Connect to Wi-Fi
d) Give to crew for inspection

Role-Play Activity Worksheet

- Topic: Pre-Departure Announcements & Checks
- Objective: Practice realistic cabin crew communication before takeoff using appropriate vocabulary, tone, and procedure.

Instructions

1. Work in pairs or small groups.
2. Assign roles (Purser / Cabin Crew / Passenger / Flight Deck).
3. Read your situation carefully.
4. Use the sample expressions or create your own based on what you learned.
5. After practicing, switch roles and repeat the scene.

Role-Play Scenarios

Role-Play 1: Welcome and Safety Announcement
- Roles: Purser, Cabin Crew, Passengers (optional)
- Scenario: You are preparing for departure. The purser makes a welcome and safety announcement.
- Task:
1. Deliver the full announcement over the PA system.
2. Cabin crew demonstrate the safety equipment during the announcement.

Unit 05. Pre-Departure Announcements & Checks

Expressions to use:
- Welcome onboard Flight ___ bound for ___.
- Please stow your carry-on items.
- We will now demonstrate the safety features of this aircraft.
- Give us your full attention.

Role-Play 2: Final Cabin Check - Passenger Non-Compliance
- Roles: Cabin Crew, Passenger
- Scenario: A passenger has not fastened their seatbelt and is using their tray table.
- Task:
1. Politely ask the passenger to comply with safety instructions.
2. Correct multiple issues: seatbelt, seatback, tray table, bag location.

Expressions to use:
- May I ask you to fasten your seatbelt?
- Please return your seat to the upright position.
- Kindly stow your tray table.
- Your bag must be fully under the seat.

Role-Play 3: Door Arming and Cross-Check
- Roles: Purser, Cabin Crew (2 positions)
- Scenario: After the boarding is complete, the purser gives the command to arm doors.
- Task:
1. Perform arming command and respond using correct door position phrases.
2. Cross-check procedures clearly and confidently.

Expressions to use:
- Arm doors and cross-check.
- 2L door armed and cross-checked.

- Cross-check complete.
- Thank you.

Role-Play 4: Reporting a Suspicious Item
- Roles: Cabin Crew, Purser
- Scenario: You find an unlabelled battery pack in a seat pocket.
- Task:
1. Report the issue clearly to the purser.
2. Follow the correct procedure: cabin safety bag, log, flight deck notification.

Expressions to use:
- I found a suspicious item in seat pocket ___.
- It looks damaged and has no label.
- I'll place it in the safety bag.
- I'll inform the flight deck immediately.

Role-Play 5: Reporting Cabin is Ready
- Roles: Purser, Flight Deck
- Scenario: After all checks and arming are complete, the purser reports to the flight deck.
- Task:
1. Use interphone to make a formal report.
2. Confirm cabin readiness clearly and professionally.

Expressions to use:
- Final cabin check complete.
- All doors armed and cross-checked.
- Cabin is secure and ready for departure.
- Standing by for further instructions.

Part 2

After Take-off

Unit 06. In-flight Service Preparation
Unit 07. Meal & Beverage Service
Unit 08. Dealing with Passenger Requests
Unit 09. Handling In-flight Issues

Unit 06. In-flight Service Preparation

Learning Objectives

- By the end of this unit, learners will be able to:
- Identify key tasks required for in-flight service preparation.
- Use appropriate vocabulary and expressions for galley setup and equipment checks.
- Communicate effectively with team members during pre-service coordination.
- Respond to common issues during service preparation with clarity and professionalism.

Introduction

In-flight service preparation is a crucial phase that takes place right after takeoff and before meal or beverage service begins. Cabin crew must ensure that all service items are properly loaded, organized, and safe to use. Effective communication between team members is essential to coordinate duties, manage limited space, and maintain safety and hygiene standards.

In this unit, we will explore typical service preparation routines such as galley setup, trolleys checks, item availability checks, and coordination between the forward and aft galleys. You will also learn key expressions and protocols to ensure smooth service delivery.

Useful Vocabulary

Term / Phrase	Meaning
galley	The kitchen area on board where meals and beverages are prepared
cart / trolley	A movable unit used to transport meals, drinks, and duty-free items
stock list	An inventory checklist of items loaded for in-flight service
replenish	To refill or restock items that are low or missing

• 항공운송 실무영어 Practical English for Cabin Crew

secure (equipment)	To fasten or make equipment safe for turbulence or movement
oven insert	A removable tray used to heat meals inside the galley oven
atlas box	An insulated box to keep items hot or cold
pre-set tray	A prepared tray with food and utensils for quick meal service
waste compartment (trash compartment)	A designated area to dispose of trash or used service items
galley power check	A routine check to ensure all galley electrical systems are working

Warm-Up Quiz

Part 1: Multiple Choice (Choose the best answer)

1. What is the main goal of in-flight service preparation?

a) To serve passengers immediately after boarding

b) To prepare and organize service items safely and efficiently

c) To brief passengers on the flight route

d) To prepare duty-free reports

2. Which of the following is found in the galley?

a) Lavatory

b) Cockpit door

c) Oven insert

d) Life vest

3. What should you do if the trolley is not secured properly?

a) Leave it until landing

b) Ignore and proceed with service

c) Report it to the captain

d) Secure it immediately to prevent injury

Unit 06. In-flight Service Preparation

Part 2: Fill in the Blanks

galley	stock list
secure	trolley
safety	pre-set tray

4. Before service, the crew checks the _____ to confirm the number of loaded items.
5. Please make sure the _____ is locked in place before takeoff.
6. Meals are placed on a _____ to speed up service.
7. The _____ is equipped with ovens, chillers, and storage compartments.
8. It is important to _____ all galley equipment during turbulence.

Situation 1: Galley Equipment Check Before Service

Setting:
Front galley of a long-haul international flight. The crew is preparing hot meals and beverages before beginning the in-flight service.

Characters:
- Cabin Crew 1: Galley operator responsible for hot meal preparation
- Cabin Crew 2: Assisting crew checking beverage and waste areas

Dialogue

Cabin Crew 1:
Let's double-check the ovens. Is oven 2 heating properly?
Cabin Crew 2:
Yes, oven 2 is pre-heated and the insert trays are in.
Cabin Crew 1:
Great. Can you check the chillers for the beverage carts?
Cabin Crew 2:
Sure. Both chillers are cold, and water bottles are stocked.
Cabin Crew 1:
Perfect. Don't forget to secure the trash bins before we begin.

· 항공운송 실무영어 Practical English for Cabin Crew

Cabin Crew 2:
Already done. Everything is locked and ready.

Key Vocabulary

Word / Phrase	Meaning
Pre-heated	Already warmed up in advance
Insert tray	A removable tray used in the oven
Chiller	A cooling device for storing beverages
Secure	To fasten or lock in place for safety
Trash bin	A container for collecting waste

Alternative Expressions

Original	Alternative Expression
Is oven 2 heating properly?	Is the second oven functioning as expected?
Water bottles are stocked	We've got enough water bottles loaded
Don't forget to secure the trash bins	Be sure the trash containers are safely locked
Everything is locked and ready	All equipment is secured and we're good to go
Can you check the chillers?	Could you take a look at the beverage coolers?

Situation 2: Missing Items on the Cart

Setting:
Rear galley just after takeoff. Crew is conducting inventory check before pushing the carts down the aisle.
Characters:
- Cabin Crew 1: Assigned to the rear galley
- Cabin Crew 2: Working in forward galley with access to additional stock

Dialogue

Cabin Crew 1:
We're missing apple juice on the aft cart. Did it get loaded?
Cabin Crew 2:
Let me check the stock list... It shows two packs, but I only see one.
Cabin Crew 1:
Can you check if the forward galley has an extra?
Cabin Crew 2:
Yes! There's one left here. I'll transfer it now.
Cabin Crew 1:
Thanks. Let's also double-check the cutlery sets.
Cabin Crew 2:
Copy that. I'll count them before we close the cart.

Key Vocabulary

Word / Phrase	Meaning
Stock list	List of inventory loaded for service
Aft cart	Trolley placed in the rear galley
Forward galley	Kitchen area near the front of the aircraft
Cutlery set	Utensils like fork, knife, spoon
Transfer	Move from one place to another

Alternative Expressions

Original	Alternative Expression
We're missing apple juice	There's no apple juice on this cart
I'll transfer it now	I'll bring it over right away
Let's double-check the cutlery sets	Let's make sure we have enough cutlery sets
Did it get loaded?	Was it included in the catering?
I'll count them before we close	I'll do a final count before sealing the trolley

• 항공운송 실무영어 Practical English for Cabin Crew

Situation 3: Team Coordination for Meal Service

Setting:
Mid-cabin, in front of service area curtain. The team is coordinating service zones and responsibilities before meal distribution.

Characters:
- Cabin Crew 1: Senior crew member handling front cabin rows
- Cabin Crew 2: Assigned to rear cabin service and special meals

Dialogue

Cabin Crew 1:
Let's sync before we start. I'll serve rows 1 to 15.

Cabin Crew 2:
Okay, I'll take rows 16 to the rear. Will you announce the meal options?

Cabin Crew 1:
Yes, I'll do it just before we begin service. Do we have vegetarian meals ready?

Cabin Crew 2:
Yes, they're labeled and placed on the upper rack.

Cabin Crew 1:
Great. If you run out of something, signal me and I'll restock from the forward galley.

Cabin Crew 2:
Sounds good. Let's start in two minutes.

Key Vocabulary

Word / Phrase	Meaning
sync	Coordinate and plan together
meal options	Different food choices offered to passengers
vegetarian meals	Meals without meat or animal products
upper rack	Upper shelf in the trolley or galley for storage
signal	To notify or alert someone silently or non-verbally

Unit 06. In-flight Service Preparation

Alternative Expressions

Original	Alternative Expression
Let's sync before we start	Let's coordinate before we begin
Will you announce the meal options?	Can you inform passengers of the menu choices?
Do we have vegetarian meals ready?	Are the meat-free options prepared?
Signal me and I'll restock	Let me know and I'll bring more from the front
Let's start in two minutes	We'll begin in about two minutes

Role-play Activity Sheet

Objective:
- Practice in-flight preparation procedures including equipment checks, item verification, and service coordination through realistic role-play scenarios.

Student Instructions:
1. Pair up with a classmate. Decide who plays Crew 1 and Crew 2.
2. Read the scenario and plan your conversation.
3. Use at least 3 key phrases provided.
4. Act out the dialogue in front of another team or the class.
5. Swap roles and try a different scenario.

Role-play 1: Oven Malfunction During Setup
- Setting: Front galley before meal service on an international flight
- Characters:
- Cabin Crew 1 - Responsible for hot meal preparation
- Cabin Crew 2 - Assisting with galley readiness
- Task: Oven #1 is not heating properly. Discuss how to proceed and find an alternative.

Key Phrases to Include:
- "Is the oven pre-heated?"
- "Let's try switching trays to oven 2."
- "We'll need to report this after the flight."

Role-play 2: Shortage of Beverage Items
- Setting: Rear galley just before beverage service
- Characters:
- Cabin Crew 1 – Checking rear beverage cart
- Cabin Crew 2 – Has access to additional supplies
- Task: Apple juice and tonic water are missing from the beverage cart. Solve the issue.

Key Phrases to Include:
- "Can you check the forward galley stock?"
- "Let's replace it before we start."
- "Please update the inventory list."

Role-play 3: Preparing Special Meals
- Setting: Mid-galley during final prep phase
- Characters:
- Cabin Crew 1 – Serving front rows
- Cabin Crew 2 – Handling special meal requests
- Task: Ensure vegetarian meals are correctly placed and labeled before service begins.

Key Phrases to Include:
- "Are the special meals labeled?"
- "Can we move them to the top of the cart?"
- "We should double-check with the manifest."

Wrap-up Summary
- Topic: In-flight Service Preparation

Unit 06. In-flight Service Preparation

- Part: After Takeoff Phase

Key Takeaways
- Proper galley preparation is essential to ensure smooth and safe in-flight service.
- Checking equipment (ovens, carts, beverage containers) must be done before any service begins.
- Inventory verification should include special meals, beverages, and replenishment items.
- Clear communication between crew members is necessary for successful coordination.
- Problem-solving during unexpected issues (e.g. malfunction, missing items) should be calm, proactive, and safety-focused.
- Passenger expectations depend heavily on well-organized, timely, and courteous service.

Quick Review Questions
1. What items should be checked in the galley before starting in-flight service?
2. How would you handle a situation where the oven is not heating properly?
3. Why is it important to label and organize special meals before serving?
4. What expressions can you use when asking your colleague to help restock missing items?
5. How can effective communication improve team performance during service?

에듀컨텐츠·휴피아
CH Educontents Huepia

Unit 07. Meal and Beverage Service

Learning Objectives

By the end of this unit, learners will be able to:
- Understand the procedures of in-flight meal and beverage service.
- Use appropriate English expressions when offering and serving food and drinks.
- Respond to passengers' special requests, including dietary needs and drink preferences.
- Practice natural and polite service language through situational dialogues.
- Demonstrate fluency and confidence in role-play scenarios.

Introduction

Meal and beverage service is one of the most visible aspects of in-flight hospitality. Cabin crew must provide timely, courteous, and clear communication while managing time, passenger preferences, and safety procedures. This unit focuses on the typical flow of in-flight meal and drink service and equips learners with useful expressions, dialogues, and role-play practice.

From offering meal options to handling special meal requests and alcoholic beverage service, effective communication ensures a smooth and pleasant in-flight experience for passengers.

Key Vocabulary

Vocabulary	Meaning
meal service	The process of offering, distributing, and clearing meals on board.
special meal	A pre-ordered meal for dietary, religious, or medical requirements.
cabin trolley	A wheeled cart used by crew to deliver food and beverages.

항공운송 실무영어 Practical English for Cabin Crew

beverage cart	A trolley specifically for serving drinks during the flight.
refill	Offering to fill a drink or cup again.
preference	A passenger's chosen option (e.g. chicken over beef).
out of stock	When a specific item is no longer available to serve.
tray collection	The process of gathering used meal trays from passengers.
leftovers	Food that remains uneaten after the meal.
disposable items	Single-use items like plastic cups, utensils, or napkins.

Warm-up Quiz

Instructions: Choose the correct answer for each question.

1. What is the first thing to check before serving alcoholic drinks?

a) Whether the passenger is hungry

b) The passenger's age and airline policy

c) The location of the beverage cart

d) The cabin lights

2. What should you say when clearing a passenger's tray?

a) May I take your tray?

b) Are you done yet?

c) Can I throw this away?

d) Move your tray, please.

3. What should you do if a passenger requests a special meal?

a) Ignore the request

b) Say it's not available

c) Verify and deliver the correct item

d) Ask them to take the regular meal

Unit 07. Meal & Beverage Service

Conversations

Situation 1: Offering Meal Options

Setting:
Shortly after takeoff on a 3-hour international flight. The aircraft has reached cruising altitude, and the first meal service is about to begin. Cabin crew members are moving meal carts through the economy cabin aisle. Passengers are awake and alert, ready to receive their meals. The crew must efficiently offer options like "beef" or "chicken" while managing limited supply.

Characters:
- Cabin Crew
- Passenger

Dialogue

Cabin Crew: Good afternoon. Would you prefer beef with mashed potatoes or chicken curry with rice?
Passenger: I'll take the chicken curry, please.
Cabin Crew: Certainly. Here you go. Would you like something to drink?
Passenger: Just water, please.
Cabin Crew: Still or sparkling?
Passenger: Still water.
Cabin Crew: Here's your still water. Enjoy your meal.

Key Vocabulary

Word / Phrase	Meaning
meal option	The type of meal choices offered to passengers
portion	A serving size of food provided on board
preference	A passenger's choice or liking for something
run out	To no longer have something available
economy class	The main cabin section where standard services are provided

· 항공운송 실무영어 Practical English for Cabin Crew

Alternative Expressions

Original Expression	Alternative Expression
Would you prefer beef or chicken?	What would you like for your main dish?
Here you go.	Here is your meal.
Would you like something to drink?	Can I offer you a beverage?
Just water, please.	Water will be fine, thank you.
Enjoy your meal.	Hope you enjoy your food.

Situation 2: Handling a Missing Meal Request

Setting:
During the main meal service in the mid-cabin zone. A passenger raises their hand to inform the crew that they pre-ordered a vegetarian special meal, but it is not available on the trolley. The crew must quickly check the manifest, apologize, and offer an appropriate solution to ensure passenger satisfaction and compliance with service standards.

Characters:
- Cabin Crew
- Passenger

Dialogue

Passenger: Excuse me. I requested a gluten-free meal.
Cabin Crew: Let me double-check the list. ···I'm sorry, I don't see your name on the special meals list.
Passenger: Oh no. I definitely selected it online.
Cabin Crew: I apologize for the inconvenience. I'll see if we have an extra gluten-free option available.
Passenger: I'd appreciate that.
Cabin Crew: Thank you for your patience. I'll be right back.

Unit 07. Meal & Beverage Service

Key Vocabulary

Word / Phrase	Meaning
special meal	A pre-ordered meal based on dietary, medical, or religious needs
manifest	An official list of passengers and special meal requests
unavailable	Not present or not provided at the moment
apologize	To express regret for a mistake or inconvenience
alternative	A different option offered in place of the original

Alternative Expressions

Original Expression	Alternative Expression
Let me double-check the list.	I'll check the list one more time.
I don't see your name on the special meals list.	Your name doesn't appear on the special request.
I apologize for the inconvenience.	I'm really sorry about the trouble.
I'll be right back.	I'll return shortly.
Thank you for your patience.	I appreciate you waiting.

Situation 3: Offering Beverages

Setting:
Following the completion of meal distribution, the cabin crew prepares a separate beverage cart to offer drinks. This service is conducted while passengers are still eating or have just finished. The crew must ask each passenger about their beverage preference—ranging from juice and soda to hot coffee or tea—while monitoring for special requests like decaf or no ice.

Characters:
- Cabin Crew
- Passenger

Dialogue
Cabin Crew: Hello again. Would you like a beverage?

Passenger: What do you have?
Cabin Crew: We have coffee, tea, juice, soda, beer, and wine.
Passenger: I'll have a cup of tea, please.
Cabin Crew: Certainly. Do you take sugar or milk with your tea?
Passenger: Just sugar, please.
Cabin Crew: Here's your tea with sugar. Enjoy.

Key Vocabulary

Word / Phrase	Meaning
beverage	A drink, such as coffee, tea, juice, or soda
soft drink	A non-alcoholic, carbonated drink like cola or lemonade
hot drink	A warm beverage such as tea or coffee
refill	To fill a cup again after it has been emptied
decaffeinated	A drink with the caffeine removed

Alternative Expressions

Original Expression	Alternative Expression
Would you like a beverage?	Can I get you something to drink?
What do you have?	What options are available?
I'll have a cup of tea, please.	Tea for me, thank you.
Do you take sugar or milk?	Would you like any sugar or milk with that?
Here's your tea with sugar.	Your tea with sugar is ready.

Situation 4: Offering Second Service

Setting:
Approximately 1.5 hours into a medium-haul flight. After the first meal, the crew prepares a second service consisting of light snacks (e.g. muffins, sandwiches, fruit cups). This is especially common on flights longer than 4 hours. The service is less formal but still follows safety and hygiene protocols. The setting is calmer, with many passengers resting or watching

Unit 07. Meal & Beverage Service

in-flight entertainment.
Characters:
- Cabin Crew
- Passenger

Dialogue

Cabin Crew: Hello, we're offering a light snack now. Would you like a sandwich or a muffin?
Passenger: I'll take the muffin, please.
Cabin Crew: Certainly. And would you like juice or coffee to go with that?
Passenger: Juice, please.
Cabin Crew: Apple or orange juice?
Passenger: Orange, please.
Cabin Crew: Here's your muffin and orange juice. Let me know if you need anything else.

Key Vocabulary

Word / Phrase	Meaning
light snack	A small meal or food item served between main meals
distribute	To hand out food or drinks to passengers
sandwich	A food item made of bread and filling, often served cold
muffin	A small, sweet cake typically served as a snack
fruit cup	A small serving of assorted fruits in a container

Alternative Expressions

Original Expression	Alternative Expression
We're offering a light snack.	We have a snack service now.
Would you like a sandwich or a muffin?	Which would you prefer, a sandwich or a muffin?
To go with that	Along with that
Apple or orange juice?	Would you like apple or orange juice?

· 항공운송 실무영어 Practical English for Cabin Crew

| Let me know if you need anything else. | Just call me if you need anything more. |

Situation 5: Collecting Meal Trays

Setting:
About 20-30 minutes after the meal service. The crew begins collecting used trays from front to back in each cabin section. Some passengers are still finishing their meals while others are ready to dispose of leftovers. Crew must communicate politely and efficiently, offering help with trash and thanking passengers for their cooperation while maintaining cabin cleanliness and speed.

Characters:
- Cabin Crew
- Passenger

Dialogue

Cabin Crew: May I clear your tray?
Passenger: Yes, I've finished. Thank you.
Cabin Crew: You're welcome. Was everything okay with your meal?
Passenger: Yes, it was good.
Cabin Crew: I'm glad to hear that. Would you like some coffee or tea now?
Passenger: No, thank you. I'll just rest for a bit.
Cabin Crew: Of course. Please let me know if you need anything.

Key Vocabulary

Word / Phrase	Meaning
tray	A flat container used to serve or collect meals
dispose	To throw away or discard items properly
rubbish	Trash or waste left after a meal
leftover	Uneaten food remaining after a meal
sanitize	To clean thoroughly to maintain hygiene

Unit 07. Meal & Beverage Service

Alternative Expressions

Original Expression	Alternative Expression
May I clear your tray?	Can I take your tray away?
Was everything okay with your meal?	Did you enjoy your meal?
I'm glad to hear that.	That's great to know.
Would you like some coffee or tea?	Can I get you a hot drink?
Please let me know if you need anything.	Feel free to call me if you need assistance.

Situation 6: Managing a Passenger Complaint About Food Quality

Setting:
During meal service, a passenger expresses dissatisfaction with the food quality (e.g. taste, temperature, appearance). The crew must stay calm, listen actively, offer a sincere apology, and if possible, provide a replacement or alternative item. This situation tests emotional intelligence and service recovery skills.

Characters:
- Cabin Crew
- Passenger

Dialogue

Cabin Crew: Excuse me, sir. Is everything alright with your meal?
Passenger: Actually, no. My chicken is really dry and cold. It's not very appetizing.
Cabin Crew: I'm very sorry to hear that. Let me see what I can do. Would you prefer the beef option instead?
Passenger: If it's available, yes.
Cabin Crew: I'll check with the galley and bring it right over if possible. Again, I truly apologize for the inconvenience.
Passenger: Thank you.
Cabin Crew: Thank you for your patience. I'll be back shortly.

· 항공운송 실무영어 Practical English for Cabin Crew

Key Vocabulary

Word	Meaning
complaint	A statement that something is unsatisfactory
appetizing	Looking or smelling good enough to eat
dry (food)	Lacking moisture, often unappealing
alternative meal	A different food option provided instead
apologize	To say sorry for a mistake or problem

Alternative Expressions

Original	Alternative Expression
I'm very sorry to hear that.	I truly apologize for the inconvenience.
Let me see what I can do.	I'll try to find a solution for you.
Would you prefer the beef option instead?	Would you like to try our other choice?
I'll check with the galley.	I'll go to the galley and see what's available.
Thank you for your patience.	I appreciate your understanding.

Situation 7: Handling a Spillage Incident During Meal Service

Setting:
While serving a hot drink or moving the trolley, a beverage is accidentally spilled on a passenger's tray table, clothes, or seat area. The crew must respond immediately with a clean-up kit, offer assistance, and apologize sincerely while following safety and customer service protocols.

Characters:
- Cabin Crew
- Passenger

Dialogue

Cabin Crew: Oh! I'm terribly sorry, sir. I accidentally spilled some coffee on your tray.

Passenger: It's okay, but my pants are wet now.

Cabin Crew: I completely understand. Let me get some tissues and a towel right away.

Unit 07. Meal & Beverage Service

Passenger: Alright.
Cabin Crew: Here you go. I'll also bring you a complimentary drink as an apology.
Passenger: That's kind. Thank you.
Cabin Crew: Once again, I sincerely apologize for the spill.

Key Vocabulary

Word	Meaning
spill	To accidentally drop a liquid
towel	A piece of cloth used for drying
complimentary	Given for free as a courtesy
sincere	Honest and heartfelt
clean-up	The process of removing dirt or mess

Alternative Expressions

Original	Alternative Expression
I'm terribly sorry.	I sincerely apologize.
Let me get some tissues and a towel.	I'll bring something to help clean it up.
I completely understand.	I see how frustrating this must be.
I'll also bring you a complimentary drink.	Please allow me to offer you a free beverage.
That's kind. Thank you.	I appreciate your gesture.

Situation 8: Refusing Alcohol to an Intoxicated Passenger

Setting:
Later in the flight, a passenger asks for more alcoholic drinks but shows signs of intoxication. The crew must politely yet firmly refuse the request, explain the policy, and de-escalate the situation without causing confrontation or embarrassment.

Characters:
- Cabin Crew
- Passenger

항공운송 실무영어 Practical English for Cabin Crew

Dialogue

Passenger: Can I have another whiskey, please?
Cabin Crew: Sir, for your safety and comfort, I'm afraid I can't serve you any more alcohol at this time.
Passenger: Come on, just one more. I'm fine.
Cabin Crew: I understand, but we have a safety policy in place. May I offer you a soft drink or water instead?
Passenger: Hmm… okay, I'll take water.
Cabin Crew: Thank you for your understanding.

Key Vocabulary

Word	Meaning
intoxicated	Affected by alcohol, not sober
policy	An official rule or guideline
refuse	To say no to a request
escalate	To become more serious or intense
soft drink	A non-alcoholic carbonated beverage

Alternative Expressions

Original	Alternative Expression
I'm afraid I can't serve you more alcohol.	I'm sorry, but I must follow our safety policy.
Just one more. I'm fine.	I feel okay—can't I just have one more?
We have a safety policy in place.	Our regulations don't allow further service.
May I offer you a soft drink instead?	Would you like some juice or water instead?
Thank you for your understanding.	I appreciate your cooperation.

Unit 07. Meal & Beverage Service

Role-play Activity Sheet

Instructions for Students:
1. Pair up with a classmate. Take turns practicing both roles.
2. Focus on tone, politeness strategies, and natural expressions.
3. After each roleplay, discuss how the situation was handled.
4. Bonus: Try changing the ending – What if the passenger becomes angry? What if another passenger gets involved?

Situation 1: Special Meal Request Not Loaded
- Setting: Economy cabin during meal service
- Roles:
1. Cabin Crew: Politely explain the missing vegetarian meal and offer an alternative
2. Passenger: Frustrated but open to solutions

Goal:
Resolve the situation by offering a suitable alternative and maintaining a positive passenger experience.

Useful Phrases:
- "I sincerely apologize for the inconvenience."
- "Let me check what other meal options we have available."
- "Would you be open to a seafood or chicken meal instead?"

Vocabulary Box:
- Vegetarian meal
- Option unavailable
- Substitute
- Inconvenience
- Apologize

• 항공운송 실무영어 Practical English for Cabin Crew

Situation 2: Beverage Refill Request
- Setting: Mid-flight after meal service, beverage cart round
- Roles:
1. Cabin Crew: Takes refill request
2. Passenger: Politely asks for another drink

Goal:
- Handle the request professionally, confirm passenger satisfaction, and offer service politely.

Useful Phrases:
- "Would you like a refill of the same drink?"
- "Certainly, I'll bring it right away."
- "Please enjoy. Let me know if you need anything else."

Vocabulary Box:
- Refill
- Soft drink
- Sparkling water
- Beverage cart
- Courtesy

Situation 3: Food Quality Complaint
- Setting: During meal service, a passenger is not satisfied with their meal
- Roles:
1. Cabin Crew: Responds to complaint and offers a solution
2. Passenger: Politely expresses dissatisfaction

Goal:
- Calm the passenger, apologize, and suggest possible actions.

Unit07. Meal & Beverage Service

🌐 Useful Phrases:
- "I'm sorry to hear that the meal didn't meet your expectations."
- "Would you like to try a different option?"
- "We appreciate your feedback and will report this."

🌐 Vocabulary Box:
- Taste
- Quality
- Unpleasant
- Apologize
- Feedback

■ **Situation 4: Refusing Alcohol Politely**
- Setting: Passenger requests another alcoholic drink but appears intoxicated
- Roles:
1. Cabin Crew: Notices signs of intoxication and refuses politely
2. Passenger: Requests more alcohol and reacts emotionally

🌐 Goal:
- Refuse politely while maintaining safety and professionalism

🌐 Useful Phrases:
- "For your safety, I can't serve more alcohol at the moment."
- "Would you like some water or juice instead?"
- "Thank you for your understanding."

🌐 Vocabulary Box:
- Intoxicated
- Safety
- Refusal
- Responsible service
- Alternative drink

Comprehension Check

[Part A. True or False]

Read the following statements and write T (True) or F (False).

	Statement	T / F
1	A passenger requests a vegetarian meal, and the cabin crew immediately finds one without checking the list.	
2	The beverage cart is used only after the meal trays have been collected.	
3	Cabin crew should avoid offering any alternative options when the requested meal is out of stock.	
4	Refusing alcohol to an intoxicated passenger should be done politely and professionally.	
5	It is acceptable for crew to ignore minor spills during the service.	

[Part B. Multiple Choice]

Choose the best answer for each question.

1. **What should a cabin crew member do first when a passenger complains about food quality?**

   a) Argue with the passenger

   b) Offer compensation immediately

   c) Listen calmly and apologize

   d) Ignore and continue service

2. **If a passenger orders a special meal that was not loaded, what should the crew do?**

   a) Apologize and offer available options

   b) Tell the passenger to wait

   c) Say it's not their fault

   d) Avoid eye contact and move on

3. What is the proper action after a spill on a passenger's seat?

a) Blame turbulence

b) Clean the area and offer assistance

c) Call the captain

d) Do nothing unless the passenger complains

4. Which of the following is a polite way to refuse an alcoholic drink to a passenger who appears intoxicated?

a) "You've had enough."

b) "Sorry, I can't give you any more alcohol."

c) "I'm afraid I can't serve you more alcohol for your safety."

d) "No more drinks for you."

5. What item is typically used to serve both food and drinks during service?

a) Luggage cart

b) Cabin trolley

c) Emergency kit

d) Trash bin

[Part C. Short Answer]

Answer the questions in a sentence or phrase.

1. What should the crew say if a meal option is no longer available?

→

2. How can the crew express appreciation when another passenger agrees to change seats for a meal-related reason?

→

3. What should the crew do before offering a refill on a passenger's drink?

→

에듀컨텐츠·휴피아
ECH Educontents Huepia

UNIT 08. Dealing with Passenger Requests

Learning Objectives

By the end of this unit, students will be able to:
- Understand common types of passenger requests during flight.
- Respond politely and clearly to a range of passenger needs.
- Use appropriate vocabulary and expressions for customer service situations.
- Practice handling multiple requests under pressure while maintaining professionalism.

Introduction

Cabin crew members are constantly approached by passengers with various needs during the flight. These requests may include asking for a blanket, switching seats, adjusting the air vent, reporting a problem, or inquiring about arrival time.

Responding to these requests effectively is a vital part of delivering excellent in-flight service. It requires active listening, clear communication, and a polite, helpful attitude. In this unit, you will learn how to handle these requests in English with confidence and professionalism.

Key Vocabulary

Vocabulary	Meaning
blanket	a soft cover used to keep warm
headset	a device worn over ears to listen to audio
seat switch	changing a seat with another passenger
overhead bin	storage compartment above the seats
air vent	a small outlet to control air flow
motion sickness	feeling ill from movement, such as in flight
assistance	help or support
available	ready to use or not occupied
adjust	to change something slightly to improve it
turbulence	irregular motion in the air during a flight

• 항공운송 실무영어 Practical English for Cabin Crew

Useful Expressions

Situation	Useful Expressions
Passenger requests something	Certainly, I'll bring that for you. Let me check if we have it available.
Passenger asks about arrival	We are expected to arrive in approximately two hours.
Passenger requests to change seat	Let me see if there's an available seat.
Passenger complains politely	I'm sorry to hear that. Let me assist you.
Offering help	Is there anything else I can help you with?
Unable to fulfill a request	I'm afraid that's not possible at the moment, but…

Warm-up Quiz

Part 1. Multiple Choice (Choose the best answer)

Choose the most appropriate response for each passenger request.

1. A passenger asks, "Can I have another blanket?"

a) "No, we're out."

b) "Maybe later."

c) "Sure, I'll bring you one right away."

2. A passenger says, "The air vent above me isn't working."

a) "So what?"

b) "Let me take a look and adjust it for you."

c) "I don't know what to do."

3. A passenger says, "Can I move to that empty seat?"

a) "That's not your seat."

b) "Please wait while I check if it's available."

c) "I don't care."

 Unit 08. Dealing with Passenger Requests

4. A passenger requests a headset. What do you say?

a) "It's not free."

b) "I'll bring you one in just a moment."

c) "Go find one yourself."

5. A passenger says, "I feel dizzy."

a) "You should've stayed home."

b) "Would you like some water or help from the crew?"

c) "I'm not a doctor."

Part 2. Word Match Activity

Match each word on the left with its correct meaning on the right by writing the corresponding letter.

No	Vocabulary	Match	Definition
1.	Blanket	___	a) to change something slightly
2.	Headset	___	b) a soft cover used to keep warm
3.	Adjust	___	c) a place to store carry-on bags above seats
4.	Overhead bin	___	d) device for listening to audio
5.	Motion sickness	___	e) feeling ill due to movement in travel
6.	Available	___	f) ready for use or not occupied
7.	Assistance	___	g) support or help
8.	Seat switch	___	h) changing seats with another passenger
9.	Turbulence	___	i) unsteady air movement during flight
10.	Air vent	___	j) outlet that controls airflow above seat

• 항공운송 실무영어 Practical English for Cabin Crew

Conversations

Situation 1: Asking for a Blanket

Setting:
During a long-haul flight, the cabin lights are dimmed and the temperature is slightly cool. A passenger begins to feel cold and presses the call button.

Characters:
- Cabin Crew
- Passenger

Dialogue

Passenger: Excuse me. I'm feeling a bit cold. Would it be possible to get a blanket?
Cabin Crew: Absolutely. I'll bring one for you right away.
Passenger: Thank you so much. That's very kind.
Cabin Crew: My pleasure. Would you like a hot drink as well to warm up?
Passenger: Yes, tea would be perfect.
Cabin Crew: Great. I'll return shortly with both items.
Passenger: Thanks again.
Cabin Crew: Here's your blanket and your tea. Be careful, it's hot.
Passenger: Thank you very much.
Cabin Crew: You're welcome. Please let me know if you need anything else.

Key Vocabulary

Word	Meaning
blanket	A soft cover used to keep warm
cold	Low temperature feeling
kind	Being nice or considerate
hot drink	A warm beverage like tea or coffee
return	To come back

Unit 08. Dealing with Passenger Requests

Alternative Expressions

Original Expression	Alternative Expression
Would it be possible to get a blanket?	Could I have a blanket, please?
I'll bring one for you right away.	I'll get you one right now.
That's very kind.	That's really thoughtful.
Would you like a hot drink?	Can I get you something warm to drink?
Please let me know if you need anything.	Feel free to ask for anything else.

Situation 2: Requesting to Change Seats

Setting:
A passenger realizes they are not comfortable in their current seat. They wish to move closer to their travel companion or change to an aisle seat.

Characters:
- Cabin Crew
- Passenger

Dialogue

Passenger: Hi, sorry to bother you. Is it possible to change my seat?
Cabin Crew: May I ask why you'd like to change seats?
Passenger: I'm currently in the middle seat and was hoping to move to an aisle seat.
Cabin Crew: Let me check the seating chart… Yes, we have an available aisle seat two rows back. Would that work for you?
Passenger: That would be perfect. Thank you so much.
Cabin Crew: I'll help you move your belongings. Please follow me.
Passenger: Really appreciate your help.
Cabin Crew: No problem at all.

Key Vocabulary

Word	Meaning
aisle seat	A seat next to the walking path
middle seat	A seat between two others

항공운송 실무영어 Practical English for Cabin Crew

chart	A diagram or schedule
belongings	Personal items or luggage
appreciate	To be thankful for something

Alternative Expressions

Original Expression	Alternative Expression
Is it possible to change my seat?	Can I switch seats, please?
I was hoping to move to an aisle seat.	I'd prefer an aisle seat, if available.
Would that work for you?	Does that sound okay to you?
I'll help you move your belongings.	Let me assist you with your items.
Really appreciate your help.	Thank you for your assistance.

Situation 3: Asking for an Extra Snack

Setting:
Mid-flight, snacks have already been served. A passenger is still hungry and politely asks for an extra snack.

Characters:
- Cabin Crew
- Passenger

Dialogue

Passenger: Excuse me. I was wondering if I could get another snack?
Cabin Crew: Sure! Let me see what's available.
Passenger: Thank you. I didn't eat much before boarding, so I'm a bit hungry.
Cabin Crew: We still have some crackers and cookies left. Would you prefer sweet or salty?
Passenger: I'll go with salty, please.
Cabin Crew: Here you go. Let me know if you'd like anything else.
Passenger: Thank you. That really helps.
Cabin Crew: You're welcome. Enjoy!

Unit 08. Dealing with Passenger Requests

Key Vocabulary

Word / Phrase	Meaning
extra snack	an additional small food item offered to a passenger outside the main service
available	ready for use or able to be provided
before boarding	the time prior to entering the aircraft
prefer	to choose one thing over another
sweet	having a sugary taste
salty	having a taste of salt
here you go	a friendly phrase used when giving something to someone
let me know	to ask someone to inform you if they need something
enjoy	to take pleasure or satisfaction from something

Alternative Expressions

Original Expression	Alternative Expression
I was wondering if I could get another snack.	Could I have one more snack?
I'm a bit hungry.	I'm still feeling a little hungry.
Would you prefer sweet or salty?	Do you want something sweet or something salty?
Here you go.	Here it is for you.
That really helps.	I appreciate it a lot.

Situation 4: Asking for Help with Overhead Bin

Setting:
After takeoff, a passenger wants to access their bag in the overhead compartment but is having trouble reaching it.

Characters:
- Cabin Crew
- Passenger

• 항공운송 실무영어 Practical English for Cabin Crew

Dialogue

Passenger: Excuse me, I can't quite reach my bag in the overhead bin. Can you help me?
Cabin Crew: Of course. Which one is yours?
Passenger: The black backpack just above row 18.
Cabin Crew: Got it. Let me bring it down for you.
Passenger: Thank you so much. I just need to grab my medication.
Cabin Crew: No problem. Just let me know when you're finished so I can store it safely again.
Passenger: Will do. I appreciate your help.
Cabin Crew: Anytime.

Key Vocabulary

Word	Meaning
Reach	To stretch to get something
Overhead bin	A storage area above the seats in an airplane
Backpack	A type of bag carried on the back
Medication	Medicine
Store	To put something away safely

Alternative Expressions

Original Expression	Alternative Expression
Can't quite reach my bag	I'm having trouble getting my bag
Let me bring it down for you.	I'll take it down for you.
I just need to grab my medication.	I need to get my medicine quickly.
Let me know when you're finished.	Tell me once you're done.
I appreciate your help.	Thanks a lot for assisting me.

Situation 5: Asking for a Pillow

Setting:
It's a long flight and passengers are getting ready to sleep. One passenger wants to be more comfortable and requests a pillow.

Characters:
- Cabin Crew
- Passenger

 Unit 08. Dealing with Passenger Requests

Dialogue

Passenger: Hi there. Do you have any extra pillows available?
Cabin Crew: Let me check… Yes, I have one right here.
Passenger: Thank you. I've been having trouble sleeping without neck support.
Cabin Crew: I understand. Would you also like a blanket or anything else to help you rest?
Passenger: I'm okay for now. Just the pillow is perfect.
Cabin Crew: Here you go. Let me know if you change your mind.
Passenger: Thanks again for being so helpful.
Cabin Crew: You're very welcome.

Key Vocabulary

Word	Meaning
Pillow	A soft cushion for the head
Neck support	Something that helps keep the neck comfortable
Rest	To relax or sleep
Trouble	Difficulty
Extra	More than the usual amount

Alternative Expressions

Original Expression	Alternative Expression
Do you have any extra pillows?	Could I get a pillow, please?
I've been having trouble sleeping.	I'm finding it hard to sleep.
Just the pillow is perfect.	The pillow alone is fine, thanks.
Let me know if you change your mind.	If you need anything later, just let me know.
Thanks again for being so helpful.	I really appreciate your kindness.

• 항공운송 실무영어 Practical English for Cabin Crew

Comprehension Check

▶ Instructions

Answer the following questions to review what you've learned. You may work individually or in pairs. Choose the best option, fill in the blanks, and match appropriately.

Part 1. Multiple Choice (Choose the best answer)

1. What is the most appropriate way for a cabin crew to respond when a passenger asks for a pillow?
   A. "That's not my job."
   B. "We don't give out pillows."
   C. "Of course. I'll bring one for you right away."
   D. "Ask someone else."

2. A passenger says, "I feel cold." What would be the BEST response?
   A. "It's not that cold in here."
   B. "Would you like a blanket or a hot drink?"
   C. "I'm cold too."
   D. "Sorry, we ran out."

3. What should the crew do first when a passenger requests to change seats?
   A. Tell the passenger to wait until landing
   B. Say no immediately
   C. Check the seating chart for availability
   D. Ignore the request

Part 2. Fill in the Blank

4. "Could you please help me with the _____ bin?"

5. "Would you like something _____ to drink with that snack?"

Unit 08. Dealing with Passenger Requests

Part 3. Match the Request with the Response

Passenger Request	Appropriate Crew Response
a. "Can I get another snack?"	1. "Let me see what's available."
b. "Can I switch to an aisle seat?"	2. "Let me check the seating chart."
c. "It's a bit cold in here."	3. "I'll bring you a blanket."
d. "I can't reach my bag."	4. "Let me assist you with that."

Answer Key

a → _____   c → _____
b → _____   d → _____

Part 4. Situational Response

6. You are a flight attendant. A passenger says:

"Excuse me, I'm having trouble sleeping. Do you have anything that might help?"

Write one possible polite response in complete sentence:
→ _____

Part 5. Vocabulary Check - Word Match

Word	Meaning
1. Blanket	a. to help someone
2. Aisle seat	b. a soft item to stay warm
3. Assist	c. a seat next to the walkway
4. Snack	d. a small item to eat between meals

Answer Key

1 → _____   3 → _____
2 → _____   4 → _____

• 항공운송 실무영어 Practical English for Cabin Crew

Role-play Activity Worksheet

Unit 08: Dealing with Passenger Requests

▶ Instructions

Work with a partner. One student will act as Cabin Crew, and the other as a Passenger. Read the setting, use the suggested expressions, and practice the dialogue naturally. Switch roles after each scenario.

Situation 1: Asking for a Blanket

- Setting: It's a night flight and the cabin is cold. The passenger wants a blanket.
1. Passenger: Ask for a blanket. Mention you're feeling cold.
2. Cabin Crew: Respond politely. Offer a hot drink if needed.

⊕ Useful expressions:

- "Would it be possible to get a blanket?"
- "I'll bring one right away."
- "Would you like something warm to drink as well?"

Situation 2: Requesting to Change Seats

- Setting: The passenger is in a middle seat and wants to switch to an aisle seat.
1. Passenger: Ask to change seats. Give a reason (comfort, motion sickness, etc.)
2. Cabin Crew: Check availability and respond appropriately.

⊕ Useful expressions:

- "Is it possible to switch seats?"
- "I'd prefer an aisle seat."
- "Let me check what's available."

Unit 08. Dealing with Passenger Requests

Situation 3: Asking for an Extra Snack
- Setting: Snack service has ended, but the passenger is still hungry.
1. Passenger: Politely ask for another snack. Explain your reason.
2. Cabin Crew: Check remaining stock and offer choices.

Useful expressions:
- "Could I get another snack, please?"
- "We have some cookies and crackers left."
- "Would you like sweet or salty?"

Situation 4: Requesting Help with Overhead Bin
- Setting: The passenger can't reach their bag stored above.
1. Passenger: Ask for help to get your bag from the overhead bin.
2. Cabin Crew: Assist politely. Remind about safety if needed.

Useful expressions:
- "I can't reach my bag. Could you help me?"
- "Let me bring it down for you."
- "Let me know when you're done so I can store it again."

Situation 5: Asking for a Pillow
- Setting: The passenger is trying to sleep and needs more neck support.
1. Passenger: Ask for a pillow and explain your discomfort.
2. Cabin Crew: Provide one and ask if the passenger needs anything else.

Useful expressions:
"Do you have an extra pillow?"
"I've been having trouble sleeping."
"Would you like a blanket as well?"

UNIT 09. Handling In-Flight Issues

Learning Objectives

By the end of this unit, students will be able to:
- Understand common in-flight issues that may arise during a flight.
- Use appropriate and professional language to respond to passenger complaints and problems.
- Demonstrate empathy and problem-solving skills through role-play and dialogues.
- Apply useful expressions when managing unexpected or stressful situations on-board.

Introduction

Cabin crew members are not only service providers but also problem solvers. During a flight, unexpected issues such as seat malfunctions, passenger complaints, lavatory problems, and noise disturbances may occur. Handling these issues quickly, calmly, and with care is essential to maintaining passenger satisfaction and safety. In this unit, we will explore common in-flight issues and how to address them professionally using English expressions that show empathy and control.

Key Vocabulary

Word / Phrase	Definition
complaint	An expression of dissatisfaction or annoyance
malfunction	A failure to function properly
discomfort	A feeling of physical or emotional unease
disturbance	Something that interrupts comfort or order
empathy	The ability to understand and share another's feelings
resolve	To solve a problem or settle a dispute
alternative	A different option or choice
apologize	To say sorry for a mistake or problem
turbulence	Sudden, violent movement of air in a flight
reassure	To comfort or reduce worry

• 항공운송 실무영어 Practical English for Cabin Crew

Useful Expressions
- I understand your concern. Let me see what I can do.
- I truly apologize for the inconvenience.
- We'll try our best to resolve this as quickly as possible.
- Would you like to move to a different seat if one is available?
- Unfortunately, the lavatory is temporarily out of service.
- Thank you for your patience.
- Please let me know if there's anything else I can help you with.
- We're currently experiencing some turbulence. Please remain seated.
- I'll inform the senior crew member and follow up shortly.
- May I offer you a drink while you wait?

Warm-Up Quiz

Part 1: Multiple Choice (Choose the Best Answer)

1. What is the best first response to a passenger complaint?

a) Tell them to calm down

b) Ignore and walk away

c) Listen carefully and apologize

d) Ask them to complain after landing

2. If a lavatory is out of service, what should you say?

a) "Try another one, I guess."

b) "It's broken. Don't use it."

c) "Just wait."

d) "I'm sorry, this lavatory is temporarily unavailable. Please use the one in the rear."

3. What expression shows empathy?

a) "It's not my fault."

b) "I understand how you feel."

c) "That's your problem."
d) "Can you be patient?"

Part 2: Word Match (Vocabulary Review)

Match the words in Column A with the correct definitions in Column B.

Words(A)	Definitions(B)
1. malfunction	a) A situation causing annoyance or discomfort
2. reassure	b) A failure to work properly
3. complaint	c) To comfort and reduce anxiety or worry
4. alternative	d) A different option
5. disturbance	e) Expression of dissatisfaction

Part 3: Fill in the Blanks

Complete the sentences with the correct word from the box below:

| turbulence | empathy | apologize |
| disturbance | resolve | inconvenience |

1. I sincerely _____ for the seat malfunction.
2. Let me try to _____ the issue as quickly as possible.
3. Showing _____ is key when dealing with complaints.
4. We're experiencing some _____. Please remain seated.
5. Sorry for the _____, we appreciate your patience.

Situation 1: Handling a Seat Malfunction

Setting:
A passenger reports that their seat won't recline during a long-haul flight. The flight attendant needs to respond politely and offer a solution.
Characters:
- Cabin Crew
- Passenger

• 항공운송 실무영어 Practical English for Cabin Crew

Dialogue

Passenger: Excuse me, my seat doesn't recline. It's stuck in the upright position.
Cabin Crew: I'm sorry to hear that. Let me take a quick look.
Passenger: I've tried the button a few times, but nothing happens.
Cabin Crew: Thank you for letting me know. Unfortunately, it seems the mechanism is not functioning properly.
Passenger: Oh… that's a bit uncomfortable for a long flight.
Cabin Crew: I completely understand. I'll check if there's an available seat we can move you to. If not, I can provide an extra pillow and blanket for your comfort.
Passenger: That would be helpful. Thanks.
Cabin Crew: My pleasure. I'll be right back with an update.

Key Vocabulary

Word	Definition
recline	to tilt backward
mechanism	a system of parts that operates a device
functioning	operating correctly
uncomfortable	not physically relaxed
available	free to use or unoccupied

Alternative Expressions

Original Phrase	Alternative Expression
I'm sorry to hear that.	I apologize for the inconvenience.
Let me take a quick look.	Let me check it for you.
It seems the mechanism is not functioning properly.	It looks like the seat is out of order.
I completely understand.	I understand how frustrating that must be.
I'll be right back with an update.	I'll return shortly with some information.

Unit 09. Handling In-flight Issues

Situation 2: Calming a Crying Child

Setting:
A baby is crying loudly during the flight, and nearby passengers are becoming annoyed. The crew member checks in with the parent and assists.

Characters:
- Cabin Crew
- Passenger(Parent)

Dialogue

Cabin Crew: Hello there, I noticed your little one is having a tough time. Is there anything I can do to help?

Parent: Oh, I'm so sorry. She's teething and hasn't been sleeping well.

Cabin Crew: I completely understand. Flying can be hard on babies. Would you like some warm water or an extra blanket?

Parent: A warm bottle might calm her down.

Cabin Crew: I'll prepare one right away. If you'd like, I can check if there's a quieter area on the plane where you could walk with her.

Parent: That would be great. Thank you.

Cabin Crew: You're doing great. I'll be right back with the bottle.

Key Vocabulary

Word	Definition
teething	when a baby's teeth start to grow
quiet area	a space with less noise and people
calm down	to become more relaxed or quiet
warm bottle	a baby bottle heated to comfort baby
tough time	experiencing difficulty or stress

Alternative Expressions

Original Phrase	Alternative Expression
Is there anything I can do to help?	Would you like some assistance?
I completely understand.	I totally get it.

Flying can be hard on babies.	Traveling is stressful for little ones.
I'll prepare one right away.	I'll get that for you immediately.
You're doing great.	You're handling this really well.

Situation 3: Managing a Medical Incident

Setting:
A baby is crying loudly during the flight, and nearby passengers are becoming annoyed. The crew member checks in with the parent and assists.

Characters:
- Cabin Crew
- Passenger

Dialogue

Passenger: I'm not feeling well. I feel dizzy and lightheaded.
Cabin Crew: I'm so sorry. Please remain seated. I'll get our medical kit and notify the purser.
Passenger: Okay… I just need some air.
Cabin Crew: I'll adjust the air vent above you and get you some water.
Passenger: Thank you.
Cabin Crew: Do you have any medical conditions or medications I should be aware of?
Passenger: I have low blood pressure.
Cabin Crew: Thank you for sharing. We'll monitor you closely. Please press the call button if you feel worse.

Key Vocabulary

Word	Definition
dizzy	feeling unsteady or lightheaded
purser	head flight attendant
monitor closely	watch carefully
adjust	to change slightly for comfort
medical kit	onboard emergency health supplies

Unit 09. Handling In-flight Issues

Alternative Expressions

Original Phrase	Alternative Expression
I'm not feeling well.	I feel unwell.
I'll get our medical kit.	I'll grab the first-aid supplies.
I'll adjust the air vent above you.	Let me increase the airflow for you.
We'll monitor you closely.	We'll keep an eye on your condition.
Press the call button if you feel worse.	Let us know immediately if your symptoms grow.

Situation 4: Resolving a Noise Complaint

Setting:
A passenger complains that the group behind them is talking loudly. The crew member must address the issue without escalating conflict.

Characters:
Cabin Crew
Passenger

Dialogue

Passenger: Excuse me, I'm having trouble resting. The people behind me are too loud.

Cabin Crew: I'm really sorry for the disturbance. Let me speak with them discreetly.

Passenger: I'd appreciate that.

Cabin Crew: Of course. I'll kindly ask them to lower their voices. Thank you for your understanding.

Passenger: Thank you.

Cabin Crew: I've spoken with them and they've agreed to be quieter. Please let me know if it continues.

• 항공운송 실무영어 Practical English for Cabin Crew

Key Vocabulary

Word	Definition
disturbance	unwanted noise or interruption
discreetly	privately, without drawing attention
rest	to relax or sleep
escalate	to make a problem worse
understanding	tolerance or patience

Alternative Expressions

Original Phrase	Alternative Expression
I'm really sorry for the disturbance.	I apologize for the noise.
Let me speak with them discreetly.	I'll have a quiet word with them.
I'd appreciate that.	That would be helpful.
Thank you for your understanding.	Thanks for being patient.
Let me know if it continues.	Inform me if the issue persists.

Situation 5: Food Item is Unavailable

Setting:
A passenger requests a specific meal option that is already out of stock. The crew must offer alternatives politely.

Characters:
- Cabin Crew
- Passenger

Dialogue

Passenger: Hi, I'd like the beef lasagna, please.
Cabin Crew: I'm sorry, we've just run out of beef lasagna.
Passenger: Oh no… that was my first choice.
Cabin Crew: I completely understand. We still have the chicken pasta and the vegetarian rice bowl available.
Passenger: Hmm… I'll take the chicken pasta then.

Unit 09. Handling In-flight Issues

Cabin Crew: Excellent choice. I'll bring that right away. Would you also like a beverage with your meal?
Passenger: Yes, a ginger ale, please.
Cabin Crew: Certainly. I'll be back shortly.

Key Vocabulary

Word	Definition
run out of	to have no more remaining
available	ready to be chosen or used
first choice	preferred option
beverage	a drink, usually non-alcoholic
vegetarian	food without meat

Alternative Expressions

Original Phrase	Alternative Expression
We've just run out of beef lasagna.	I'm afraid we're out of beef lasagna.
I completely understand.	I know that must be disappointing.
We still have chicken pasta and rice.	The remaining options are chicken or veggie.
I'll bring that right away.	I'll serve it to you shortly.
I'll be back shortly.	I'll return in a moment.

Comprehension Check

Choose the Best Answer (Multiple Choice)

1. What is the flight attendant's response when a seat won't recline?

a) She tells the passenger to fix it themselves.

b) She offers to change the seat or provide comfort items.

c) She ignores the complaint.

d) She says it's not her responsibility.

2. How does the crew help a parent with a crying baby?

a) Asks them to keep quiet immediately.

· 항공운송 실무영어 Practical English for Cabin Crew

b) Gives them sleeping pills.

c) Offers warm water or a quiet area.

d) Moves the parent to the back of the plane.

3. What does the flight attendant do during a medical issue?

a) Asks the passenger to walk it off.

b) Notifies the purser and offers water.

c) Ignores the situation.

d) Offers a meal instead.

4. How is a noise complaint handled?

a) The noisy group is removed from the plane.

b) The passenger is told to ignore it.

c) The crew speaks with the group discreetly.

d) No action is taken.

5. What happens when the requested meal runs out?

a) The passenger is not given any food.

b) The crew offers alternative meal options.

c) The crew blames the passenger.

d) The crew walks away.

Complete the sentences with the correct word from the box below:

discreetly	functioning	available
bottle	purser	given

6. The seat mechanism is not _____ properly.

7. The cabin crew offered a warm _____ for the crying baby.

8. The head flight attendant is called the _____.

9. The cabin crew speaks _____ to avoid conflict.

10. The vegetarian meal is still _____ even if the beef lasagna runs out.

Unit 09. Handling In-flight Issues

Wrap-up Quiz

Part 1: Word Match (Vocabulary Review)
Match the word to its correct definition.

Word	Definition
1. turbulence	a. to make a problem go away or settle it
2. empathy	b. unexpected or rough air movement
3. resolve	c. showing understanding of someone's feelings
4. inconvenience	d. something that causes discomfort or trouble

Part 2: Choose the Best Response (Multiple Choice)
Choose the most appropriate response from a flight attendant.

1. A passenger complains that the cabin is too cold.
a) "That's not my problem."
b) "I'll let the captain know you're unhappy."
c) "I understand. Let me offer you a blanket."

2. A child is crying loudly near a sleeping passenger.
a) "There's nothing I can do about it."
b) "I'll try to speak with the parent to calm the child."
c) "Please change your seat if it bothers you."

Part 3: Fill in the Blank (Use the words below)

| apologize | delay | patience |
| disturb | seatbelt | discomfort |

1. We sincerely _____ for the delay in beverage service.
2. Thank you for your _____ and understanding.
3. Please fasten your _____ due to turbulence.

항공운송 실무영어 Practical English for Cabin Crew

Role-play Activity Worksheet

⁑ Instructions
1. Work in pairs. One person will play the cabin crew, and the other will act as the passenger.
2. Choose one of the five in-flight issue scenarios below. You may also draw a random card or be assigned one by your instructor.
3. Prepare and perform a short roleplay conversation based on the situation. The cabin crew should respond professionally and with empathy.
4. Use useful expressions and alternative phrases introduced in this unit.
5. After completing the roleplay, discuss what went well and what can be improved.

Scenarios (Choose One)

Scenario	Situation
1	Your seat won't recline, and it's a 10-hour flight.
2	Your baby keeps crying, and you feel overwhelmed.
3	You suddenly feel dizzy and lightheaded.
4	The group behind you is being noisy while you try to sleep.
5	Your meal of choice is not available.

Checklist for Cabin Crew Role
- ✓ Politely listen to the complaint
- ✓ Show empathy
- ✓ Offer a solution or alternative
- ✓ Use professional expressions
- ✓ Thank the passenger for their understanding

Unit 09. Handling In-flight Issues

Self-Reflection (After Role-play)

1. What did you do well?

2. What could you improve next time?

3. Did you use alternative expressions? Which ones?

에듀컨텐츠·휴피아
Educontents Huepia

Part 3

After Landing

Unit 10. Preparing for Landing
Unit 11. Arrival Procedures
Unit 12. Post-Flight Duties & Debriefing

UNIT 10. Preparing for Landing

Learning Objectives

By the end of this unit, students will be able to:
- Understand the standard landing preparation procedures for cabin crew.
- Communicate effectively with passengers during final descent.
- Deliver final safety instructions clearly and professionally.
- Use appropriate English expressions to ensure cabin readiness for landing.
- Handle last-minute passenger requests or concerns prior to arrival.

Introduction

Preparing for landing is one of the most critical stages of the flight. As the aircraft begins its descent, cabin crew members must ensure that passengers, the cabin environment, and service items are properly secured. This includes checking seat belts, upright seatbacks, stowing tray tables, turning off electronic devices, and giving final announcements.

Passengers may also have last-minute requests or express anxiety about landing. In such cases, cabin crew must respond with calmness, clarity, and professionalism. This unit focuses on the communication strategies and standard English expressions required during this crucial phase of flight.

Key Vocabulary

Word / Phrase	Meaning
final approach	The last part of the aircraft's flight before landing
cabin secure	Confirmation that the cabin is ready for landing
tray table	A foldable table in front of a passenger seat
upright position	The vertical position of the seatback
overhead bin	Storage compartment above passenger seats
stow	To put something away safely or neatly

• 항공운송 실무영어 Practical English for Cabin Crew

Cabin check	A final inspection of the cabin
Disarm doors	To deactivate the emergency slide system
Cross-check	Procedure to double-check safety actions
Brace position	A body posture for emergency landing

Useful Expressions

Expression	Usage
Please make sure your seat back is in the upright position.	Remind passengers to adjust seatbacks
Ensure all carry-on items are stowed either under the seat or overhead.	Instruct on proper storage of items
We'll be landing shortly. Please fasten your seat belt.	Inform passengers of imminent landing
Cabin crew, please prepare the cabin for landing.	Announcement to crew
If you need assistance, please press the call button.	Offer help during final moments
For safety reasons, all electronic devices must now be turned off.	Enforce electronic device policy

Warm-Up Quiz

Read each statement and mark it True (T) or False (F).

Statement	T/F
1. The final cabin check is completed after the plane lands.	
2. Tray tables must be folded and locked before landing.	
3. Passengers are allowed to use their laptops during the final descent.	
4. Cabin crew should instruct passengers to remain seated until the aircraft stops.	
5. Disarming doors happens before the aircraft lands.	

Unit 10. Preparing for Landing

Situation 1: Ensuring Seat Belts Are Fastened

Setting:
Final descent has been announced. A cabin crew member walks through the aisle checking seat belts.

Characters:
- Cabin Crew
- Passenger

Dialogue

Cabin Crew: Excuse me, sir. May I check your seat belt, please?
Passenger: Oh, I forgot. Let me fasten it now.
Cabin Crew: Thank you. Please keep it fastened until we arrive at the gate.
Passenger: Sure, no problem.
Cabin Crew: Also, please make sure your seat back is in the upright position.
Passenger: Like this?
Cabin Crew: Perfect. Thank you for your cooperation.

Key Vocabulary

Word / Phrase	Meaning
seat belt	A safety strap worn by passengers
fasten	To securely close or attach
upright position	Seat position during takeoff and landing
final descent	Last part of the flight before landing
aisle	Walkway between seat rows

Alternative Expressions

Original Expression	Alternative Expression
May I check your seat belt, please?	Could you confirm your seat belt is fastened?
Please keep it fastened until we arrive at the gate.	Kindly leave your seat belt on until arrival.

• 항공운송 실무영어 Practical English for Cabin Crew

Make sure your seat back is in the upright position.	Please return your seat to its upright position.
Thank you for your cooperation.	I appreciate your help.
Let me fasten it now.	I'll buckle it right away.

Situation 2: Stowing Cabin Items

Setting:
The aircraft is descending. A passenger still has a bag on their lap.

Characters:
- Cabin Crew
- Passenger

Dialogue

Cabin Crew: Ma'am, for safety reasons, please stow your bag under the seat.
Passenger: Oh, I was just about to. Sorry about that.
Cabin Crew: No problem. Let me assist you.
Passenger: Thank you.
Cabin Crew: You're welcome. Also, please make sure your tray table is locked.
Passenger: Done! Is everything okay now?
Cabin Crew: Yes, thank you very much.

Key Vocabulary

Word / Phrase	Meaning
stow	To safely store something
tray table	Foldable table attached to the seat
under the seat	Storage location in front of passenger's seat
safety reasons	Justification based on risk avoidance
assist	Help or support

Unit 10. Preparing for Landing

Alternative Expressions

Original Expression	Alternative Expression
Please stow your bag under the seat.	Kindly place your bag beneath your seat.
No problem. Let me assist you.	That's alright. I can help you with that.
Please make sure your tray table is locked.	Ensure your tray table is closed and secured.
Thank you very much.	I appreciate it.
Done! Is everything okay now?	All set. Is this alright?

Situation 3: Final Cabin Check with Crew

Setting:
Cabin crew are coordinating to complete final checks before landing.

Characters:
- Lead Cabin Crew
- Rear Cabin Crew

Dialogue

Lead Crew: Cabin ready for landing?
Rear Crew: Aft cabin is secure. Overhead bins closed, passengers seated.
Lead Crew: Tray tables and seat backs?
Rear Crew: Checked and locked. Lavatories are also vacant.
Lead Crew: Great. Disarm and cross-check after landing.
Rear Crew: Copy that.

Key Vocabulary

Word / Phrase	Meaning
aft cabin	The rear section of the aircraft
overhead bins	Storage compartments above seats
lavatories	Onboard bathrooms

항공운송 실무영어 Practical English for Cabin Crew

disarm	To deactivate slide functions of the door
cross-check	Confirming completion of a safety procedure

Alternative Expressions

Original Expression	Alternative Expression
Cabin ready for landing?	Is the cabin secured for landing?
Aft cabin is secure.	The back of the cabin is all set.
Tray tables and seat backs?	Are all tables and seats in the correct position?
Lavatories are also vacant.	Restrooms are empty as well.
Copy that.	Understood.

Situation 4: Addressing Nervous Passenger

Setting:
A passenger expresses anxiety as the plane prepares to land.

Characters:
- Cabin Crew
- Nervous Passenger

Dialogue

Passenger: Excuse me, I'm a little nervous about landing.
Cabin Crew: I understand. It's very common. Just sit back and breathe deeply.
Passenger: Is it going to be a rough landing?
Cabin Crew: The captain reported smooth weather. We'll be on the ground shortly.
Passenger: Okay. I'll try to stay calm.
Cabin Crew: You're doing great. Let me know if you need anything else.

Key Vocabulary

Word / Phrase	Meaning
Nervous	Anxious or worried

Rough landing	A landing with strong impact or turbulence
Smooth weather	Calm and stable atmospheric condition
Sit back	Relax or lean against the seat
Breathe deeply	Take long and slow breaths

Alternative Expressions

Original Expression	Alternative Expression
I'm a little nervous about landing.	I feel uneasy about the landing.
Sit back and breathe deeply.	Try to relax and take deep breaths.
We'll be on the ground shortly.	We'll be landing in just a few minutes.
I'll try to stay calm.	I'll do my best to remain composed.
Let me know if you need anything else.	Feel free to call me if you need assistance.

Situation 5: Electronic Device Reminder

Setting:
The cabin crew notices a passenger using a phone during final descent.

Characters:
- Cabin Crew
- Passenger

Dialogue

Cabin Crew: Sir, the use of mobile phones is prohibited during landing.
Passenger: I'm sorry. I'll turn it off right away.
Cabin Crew: Thank you. It's for your safety and the safety of others.
Passenger: Understood.
Cabin Crew: Also, please fasten your seat belt if you haven't done so already.
Passenger: Yes, it's fastened.

• 항공운송 실무영어 Practical English for Cabin Crew

Key Vocabulary

Word / Phrase	Meaning
prohibited	Not allowed
mobile phone	A portable communication device
turn off	Power down a device
safety of others	Protecting other passengers
fasten	Secure something (e.g. seat belt)

Alternative Expressions

Original Expression	Alternative Expression
The use of mobile phones is prohibited.	Using mobile phones is not allowed.
I'll turn it off right away.	I'll switch it off immediately.
For your safety and the safety of others.	To ensure your safety and that of fellow passengers.
Please fasten your seat belt.	Kindly make sure your seat belt is secured.
Yes, it's fastened.	It's already buckled.

Comprehension Check

Instructions

Read each question carefully and choose the best answer or write your response.

Multiple Choice

1. What should a cabin crew check before landing?

a) Tray tables are down

b) Passengers are walking

c) Seat belts are fastened

d) Overhead bins are open

Unit 10. Preparing for Landing

2. What should passengers do with their electronic devices?

a) Use freely

b) Turn off or switch to airplane mode

c) Keep them on their lap

d) Charge them during descent

3. Which item must be stowed before landing?

a) Seatbelt

b) Blanket

c) Headphones

d) Handbag

4. How should the seatback be positioned?

a) Reclined

b) Neutral

c) Upright

d) Leaning forward

5. What is the term for confirming safety procedures with another crew member?

a) Sign-off

b) Check-in

c) Cross-check

d) Recall

Wrap-up Quiz

Part 1: Multiple Choice (Choose the best answer)

1. What is the main reason for making a cabin check before landing?

a) To offer more food to passengers

b) To collect garbage

항공운송 실무영어 Practical English for Cabin Crew

c) To ensure passenger and cabin safety

d) To hand out immigration forms

2. Which announcement is usually made before landing?

a) "Duty-free service will begin shortly."

b) "We have started our descent. Please return to your seats."

c) "Cabin crew, prepare doors for departure."

d) "Passengers may now use mobile phones."

3. What should a cabin crew do if a passenger refuses to fasten their seatbelt during landing?

a) Ignore the situation

b) Ask the passenger politely and inform them of safety regulations

c) Call the captain immediately

d) Offer the passenger a snack

Part 2: Word Match – Match each word with its meaning

Vocabulary	Meaning
1. Brace position	a. Walking through the cabin to inspect
2. Cabin secure	b. Position to reduce injury during impact
3. Cabin check	c. All safety requirements are met
4. Lavatory	d. Small restroom on an aircraft
5. Overhead bin	e. Compartment above seats for baggage

Part 3: Fill in the Blanks

Complete the sentence with a correct word from the box.

fasten	return	upright
landing	tray	take-off

Unit 10. Preparing for Landing

1. Please _____ your seatbelt and make sure it is securely fastened.
2. All passengers must _____ to their seats.
3. Your seatback must be in the _____ position.
4. Please stow your _____ table before landing.
5. We are now making our final approach for _____.

Role-play Activity Worksheet

Activity Objective

To practice responding to typical passenger situations during the final descent and landing phase using appropriate language, procedures, and professional tone.

Instructions

1. Work in pairs - one student plays the Cabin Crew, and the other plays the Passenger.
2. Choose one of the scenarios below, or be assigned one by your instructor.
3. Prepare a short dialogue (about 1-2 minutes) based on the situation.
4. The Cabin Crew should use polite but firm language, appropriate useful expressions, and show situational awareness.
5. After the roleplay, use the feedback section to reflect on your performance.

Choose a Scenario

No	Scenario Description
1	A passenger is sleeping with their seat reclined and tray table down during final approach.
2	A passenger is using their mobile phone and refuses to switch it off.

3	A handbag is sticking out into the aisle. The cabin crew needs to ask the passenger to stow it properly.
4	Cabin crew performs the final cabin safety check and reports "Cabin secure, cross-check complete."
5	A nervous passenger expresses fear during the descent. The cabin crew must reassure them calmly.
6	A passenger gets up to use the lavatory while the seatbelt sign is on during descent.

Role-play Activity Example

Chosen Scenario
- Scenario No. 2 – A passenger is using their mobile phone and refuses to switch it off.

Passenger's Action/Concern
- The passenger is still using their mobile phone to send a message as the plane begins its descent, despite the announcement.

Cabin Crew's Response (2~3 Sentences)
- "Excuse me, sir. For safety reasons, all electronic devices must be turned off at this time. May I kindly ask you to switch off your phone now?"
- "If you need to finish your message, please do so quickly and then power it off. Thank you for your cooperation."

Useful Expressions Used

Expression
- For safety reasons, all electronic devices must be turned off.
- May I kindly ask you to switch off your phone now?

Was safety protocol followed?
✔ Yes

Unit 10. Preparing for Landing

Peer Feedback (1 Sentence)
- "Great job maintaining a polite and professional tone while firmly enforcing the safety rule."

Language Support - Suggested Expressions
Cabin Crew may use these expressions during the roleplay:
- "May I kindly ask you to…?"
- "For your safety, please…"
- "The seatbelt sign is on, so I must ask you to remain seated."
- "Let me help you stow that bag properly."
- "We'll be landing shortly. Please prepare for arrival."
- "I understand how you feel. It'll be over soon."

Role-play Script Template

Item	Your Notes
Chosen Scenario	Scenario No. ___
Passenger's Action/Concern	
Cabin Crew's Response (2~3 sentences)	
Useful Expressions Used (List at least 2)	
Was safety protocol followed?	Yes / No
Peer Feedback (1 sentence)	

에듀컨텐츠·휴피아
Educontents Huepia

UNIT 11. Arrival Procedures

Learning Objectives

By the end of this unit, learners will be able to:
- Understand standard procedures during aircraft arrival and taxiing.
- Deliver clear landing and farewell announcements.
- Assist transit passengers with connecting flight information.
- Maintain professional conduct during disembarkation.

Introduction

The arrival phase is the final stage of flight and includes several critical responsibilities for cabin crew members. From delivering landing announcements and disarming the doors to managing transit passengers and conducting security checks, every step must be carried out professionally and safely. Cabin crew are also the last point of contact with passengers, making the farewell greeting a key opportunity to leave a positive final impression. In this unit, we will explore real-life scenarios and useful expressions that help cabin crew perform essential arrival tasks in English.

Key Vocabulary

Word / Phrase	Meaning
Disembarkation	The process of leaving the aircraft
Taxiing	Movement of the aircraft on the ground
Connecting flight	A subsequent flight requiring transfer
Farewell announcement	A message delivered at the end of a flight
Disarm the doors	Deactivate the emergency evacuation slide system
Transit passenger	A passenger continuing on another flight
Arrival announcement	In-flight message about landing and procedures
Cabin disarm check	Safety verification after landing
Cabin lights	Lights adjusted during landing and taxiing
Arrival gate	Airport gate where passengers exit the aircraft

• 항공운송 실무영어 Practical English for Cabin Crew

Useful Expressions
- "We have just landed at [Destination]."
- "Please remain seated until the seatbelt sign is off."
- "Passengers with connecting flights, please contact ground staff."
- "Cabin crew, disarm all doors and cross-check."
- "Thank you for flying with us."

Warm-up Quiz

Part 1: Word Match

Match the term with its correct definition.

Options:

A. A procedure where crew inspects for left items after arrival
B. Moving the aircraft on the ground after landing
C. Passenger continuing on another flight
D. To disable the emergency slide before opening the door
E. To verify procedures by a second crew member

Term	A	B	C	D	E
1. Taxiing					
2. Disarm					
3. Cross-check					
4. Transit					
5. Security check					

Part 2: Fill in the Blanks

Complete the sentences with the correct words.

farewell greeting	taxiing	disarm
transit passenger	security checks	taking off

1. Please remain seated while the aircraft is _____ to the gate.

2. After arrival, the cabin crew must _____ the doors before opening.
3. The purser instructed the crew to begin the _____ _____.
4. We'd like to wish you a pleasant stay and thank you for flying with us. This is part of the _____ _____.
5. A _____ _____ is someone continuing their journey to another destination.

Situation 1: Landing Announcement (During Taxiing)

Setting:
The aircraft has just landed and is taxiing to the gate. Cabin crew must make the final arrival announcement reminding passengers to remain seated and give arrival instructions.

Characters:
- Cabin Crew (PA announcement)

Dialogue

Cabin Crew (via PA):
Ladies and gentlemen, welcome to Incheon International Airport. The local time is 3:40 p.m., and the outside temperature is 26 degrees Celsius.
For your safety, please remain seated with your seatbelt fastened until the aircraft comes to a complete stop and the seatbelt sign is turned off.
Please be careful when opening the overhead compartments, as items may have shifted during the flight.
We ask that you check your seat and surrounding area for any personal belongings before leaving.
Thank you for flying with us today. It has been our pleasure to serve you.

Key Vocabulary

Term	Definition
Taxiing	Moving the aircraft on the ground after landing

• 항공운송 실무영어 Practical English for Cabin Crew

Overhead compartments	Storage space above passenger seats
Seatbelt sign	Illuminated sign to indicate seatbelt requirement
Personal belongings	Items owned by passengers
Complete stop	When the aircraft is no longer moving

Alternative Expressions

Original Sentence	Alternative Expression
Please remain seated.	Kindly stay in your seat.
Comes to a complete stop.	Has fully stopped.
Seatbelt fastened.	Seatbelt securely fastened.
Thank you for flying with us.	We appreciate you choosing to fly with us.
Be careful when opening overhead bins.	Use caution when retrieving your belongings.

Situation 2: Disarming Doors

Setting:
After landing, before opening the aircraft doors, cabin crew must disarm the emergency slides and cross-check each other's positions.

Characters:
- Lead Cabin Crew
- Aft Cabin Crew

Dialogue

Lead Cabin Crew: Doors to arrival and cross-check.
Aft Cabin Crew (via interphone): Aft door disarmed and cross-checked.
Lead Cabin Crew: Copy that. Forward door disarmed and cross-checked as well. Waiting for the bridge to be in position.
Aft Cabin Crew: Understood. All clear in the cabin. Ready for arrival.

Key Vocabulary

Term	Definition
Disarm	To deactivate the emergency slide function
Cross-check	Verifying safety procedures with another crew member
Arrival position	Aircraft parked and ready for passenger disembarkation
Interphone	Cabin communication device
All clear	No issues; ready for next step

Alternative Expressions

Original Sentence	Alternative Expression
Doors to arrival.	Set doors to disarmed mode.
Cross-checked.	Procedure confirmed.
All clear in the cabin.	Cabin is secure.
Ready for arrival.	Standing by for passenger disembarkation.
Waiting for the bridge.	Awaiting jet bridge alignment.

Situation 3: Farewell Greeting

Setting:
Passengers are disembarking, and cabin crew stand at the doors to give parting words and ensure passengers leave safely.

Characters:
- Cabin Crew
- Passenger

Dialogue

Cabin Crew: Thank you for flying with us. Have a wonderful stay in Seoul.
Passenger: Thank you. The service was excellent.
Cabin Crew: We're so glad to hear that. Take care and we hope to see you again soon!
Passenger: Definitely. Goodbye!
Cabin Crew: Goodbye, and have a safe journey.

· 항공운송 실무영어 Practical English for Cabin Crew

Key Vocabulary

Term	Definition
Farewell	A polite way to say goodbye
Disembark	To leave the aircraft
Safe journey	A way to wish someone well when they travel
Excellent service	High-quality customer service
Take care	A warm closing expression

Alternative Expressions

Original Sentence	Alternative Expression
Thank you for flying with us.	We appreciate your choosing our airline.
Have a wonderful stay.	Enjoy your visit.
Hope to see you again soon.	We look forward to welcoming you again.
Take care.	Stay well.
Have a safe journey.	Travel safely.

Situation 4: Transit Passengers

Setting:
Some passengers are in transit and must proceed to transfer counters or gates. Cabin crew provides assistance and direction.
Characters:
- Cabin Crew
- Transit Passenger

Dialogue

Passenger: Excuse me, I have a connecting flight to Los Angeles. Do I need to go through security again?
Cabin Crew: Yes, you'll need to proceed to the transfer security checkpoint. Please follow the signs for transit passengers.
Passenger: Do I collect my luggage now?

Cabin Crew: No, your checked luggage will be transferred automatically. You just need your boarding pass and passport.
Passenger: Got it. Thank you for your help!
Cabin Crew: You're welcome. Enjoy your next flight!

Key Vocabulary

Term	Definition
Transit passenger	A traveler transferring between flights
Transfer counter	Desk for rechecking boarding or changing flights
Security checkpoint	Area where passengers are screened
Checked luggage	Baggage stored in the aircraft hold
Connecting flight	A second flight following the initial one

Alternative Expressions

Original Sentence	Alternative Expression
Follow the signs.	Please proceed according to the signage.
Your luggage will be transferred.	Your bags will be automatically routed.
Do I collect my luggage?	Should I pick up my bags now?
Got it.	Understood.
Enjoy your next flight.	Have a pleasant onward journey.

Situation 5: Security Check After Disembarkation

Setting:
After all passengers have disembarked, the cabin crew must perform a thorough cabin security check for left items or suspicious materials.

Characters:
- Purser
- Cabin Crew

· 항공운송 실무영어 Practical English for Cabin Crew

Dialogue

Purser: All passengers have disembarked. Please begin the final cabin security check.
Cabin Crew: Understood. I'll start from the aft section.
Purser: Remember to check under the seats, seat pockets, and lavatories.
Cabin Crew: Copy that. Overhead bins are clear. Found one water bottle in seat 21C.
Purser: Noted. Let's complete the checklist and report to the ground staff.

Key Vocabulary

Term	Definition
Cabin security check	Inspection for left items or hazards post-flight
Seat pocket	Storage area behind the seat
Overhead bins	Luggage compartments above the seats
Lavatory	Airplane bathroom
Ground staff	Airport personnel handling aircraft on the ground

Alternative Expressions

Original Sentence	Alternative Expression
Begin the final cabin check.	Start the post-flight inspection.
Check under the seats.	Inspect below the seats.
Overhead bins are clear.	Upper compartments have no items.
Let's complete the checklist.	Finish the inspection form.
Report to the ground staff.	Inform the airport team.

Comprehension Check

▶ Instructions

Choose the correct answer or fill in the blanks based on what you learned

Unit 11. Arrival Procedures

in this unit.

Multiple Choice

1. What should passengers do immediately after landing?

a) Stand up and take their bags

b) Remain seated with seatbelts fastened

c) Open overhead bins

d) Use the lavatory

2. What does "Doors to arrival" mean?

a) Close the doors

b) Arm the doors for emergency

c) Disarm the doors for arrival

d) Open the doors immediately

3. Which expression is appropriate when saying goodbye to passengers?

a) "See you later."

b) "Get off quickly."

c) "Have a wonderful stay."

d) "Watch your step or else."

4. Transit passengers must:

a) Stay on the plane

b) Reclaim baggage

c) Go through security again

d) Wait for final boarding call at gate

5. What should crew members do after all passengers disembark?

a) Rest in the crew lounge

b) Leave immediately

c) Conduct a cabin security check

d) Turn off all cabin lights

• 항공운송 실무영어 Practical English for Cabin Crew

Wrap-up Quiz

▶ Instructions:
Match the words to their definitions and complete the sentences with the correct terms.

Part 1. Multiple Choice (Choose the best answer)

1. What is the correct PA announcement during taxiing after landing?
a) "Please fasten your seatbelt and remain seated."
b) "Cabin crew, arm doors and cross-check."
c) "Please remain seated until the aircraft has come to a complete stop."
d) "The cabin is now ready for takeoff."

2. What does "disarming the doors" mean?
a) Locking the cabin door after landing
b) Activating the emergency slide
c) Deactivating the slide system after landing
d) Arming the slide for takeoff

3. What is the best way to say goodbye to passengers leaving the aircraft?
a) "Get off quickly, please."
b) "Thank you for flying with us. Have a great day."
c) "Come back soon, or not."
d) "Don't forget to complain if needed."

Part 2. Fill in the blanks - 3 points each

4. "Cabin crew, _____ and cross-check."

5. "Please remain _____ until the seatbelt sign is turned off."

6. "Please ensure you do not leave any _____ behind."

Part 3. Matching – Match the sentence with the correct meaning

Expressions	Meaning
A. "Doors to arrival and cross-check."	1. Thank passengers politely and professionally.
B. "We hope you enjoyed your flight."	2. Deactivate the door slide system after landing.
C. "Have a pleasant stay."	3. Express gratitude and say goodbye.

Role-play Activity Worksheet

Instructions

1. Pair up – one plays the Cabin Crew, the other a Passenger.
2. Choose one arrival-related situation from the list.
3. Use the prompts below to prepare a 2–3 minute roleplay.
4. Use authentic tone, gestures, and appropriate service expressions.
5. After the roleplay, fill out the self-reflection section.

Role-play Situations (Choose one)

No	Title	Goal for Cabin Crew
1	Landing Announcement	Deliver a clear and professional arrival announcement.
2	Disarming Doors & Cross-Check	Confirm door status and safety with fellow crew.
3	Farewell Greeting	Greet passengers warmly and ensure safe exit.
4	Transit Passenger Assistance	Help a confused passenger with their connecting flight.

• 항공운송 실무영어 Practical English for Cabin Crew

| 5 | Cabin Security Check after Disembarkation | Report findings and ensure the cabin is secure. |

Role-play Planning Table

Role	Lines to Use (at least 2)	Gesture / Tone to Practice
Cabin Crew	e.g. "Please remain seated until the aircraft has come to a complete stop."	Calm, clear, professional
	e.g. "Thank you for flying with us. Enjoy your stay."	Smile, maintain eye contact
Passenger	e.g. "Could you help me find my next gate?"	Polite, slight confusion or stress
	e.g. "Thank you for your assistance."	Friendly, appreciative

Useful Expressions

- "Doors to arrival and cross-check."
- "Please remain seated until the seatbelt sign is turned off."
- "If you have a connecting flight, please follow the transit signs."
- "We hope you enjoyed your flight."
- "Please don't forget your personal belongings."

Reflection After Role-play

Question	Your Answer
What went well during the roleplay?	
What expression felt most natural to use?	
What was challenging (e.g. tone, vocabulary)?	
One thing I want to improve next time is:	

UNIT 12. Post-flight Duties

Learning Objectives

By the end of this unit, learners will be able to:
- Follow systematic procedures for post-flight safety and cleanliness checks.
- Handle lost and found items properly and professionally.
- Complete post-flight reports and documentation.
- Participate in debriefings and crew feedback sessions.

Introduction

Even after all passengers have disembarked, cabin crew responsibilities continue. Post-flight duties include checking the cabin for cleanliness, identifying and reporting lost items, and completing required documentation. A final debriefing ensures effective communication and improvement.

Key Vocabulary

Word / Phrase	Meaning
Post-flight check	Inspection after all passengers have left
Lost and found	System for handling misplaced items
Trash collection	Gathering leftover garbage from the cabin
Debriefing	Crew discussion after the flight
Cabin inspection	Detailed check of seats, overhead bins, etc.
Passenger report form	Document for reporting in-flight incidents
Cleaning crew	Ground staff in charge of aircraft cleaning
Crew rotation	Changeover between crew teams
Duty roster	Schedule of responsibilities for crew members
Final report submission	End-of-flight documentation requirement

• 항공운송 실무영어 Practical English for Cabin Crew

Useful Expressions
- "Let's begin our post-flight check from the rear galley."
- "I found a tablet in seat 24A. Can you log it?"
- "Please complete the incident report before debriefing."
- "Is the overhead bin in row 12 cleared?"
- "Thank you for your teamwork today."

Warm-up Quiz

Part 1. Word Match

Match each word with its correct meaning by writing the correct letter next to the number.

No.	Term		Meaning
1	Taxiing		A. Process of passengers leaving the aircraft
2	Disembarkation		B. Message before or after landing
3	Arrival announcement		C. Aircraft moving on the ground
4	Transit passenger		D. Passenger connecting to another flight
5	Disarm the door		E. Make evacuation slide inactive

Part 2. Fill in the Blanks

Choose the correct word to complete each sentence.

trash	report	debriefing
cabin inspection	cleaning crew	restock

6. The _____ is responsible for tidying up the cabin.

7. Don't forget to submit the incident _____.

8. After the flight, all crew members join a _____.

Unit 12. Post-Flight Duties & Debriefing

9. A full _____ must be done after disembarkation.

10. We collected all the leftover _____ from seat pockets.

Part 3. Short Answer

Read each question carefully and write a brief but complete answer in one or two sentences. Use specific details related to post-flight duties whenever possible.

11. What should cabin crew check during the post-flight cabin inspection?

12. Why is the debriefing important after a flight?

Conversations

Situation 1: Post-flight Cabin Check

Setting:
After all passengers have disembarked, the cabin crew performs a routine inspection to ensure the cabin is clean, safe, and ready for the next flight.
Characters:
- Purser (Lead Cabin Crew)
- Cabin Crew Member

Dialogue

Purser: Let's begin the post-flight cabin check. Please start with the aft section.
Crew: Sure. I'll check the seat pockets, tray tables, and overhead bins.
Purser: Don't forget to inspect the lavatories and galley as well.
Crew: Understood. If I find any suspicious or damaged items?
Purser: Report them immediately. Safety first.
Crew: Got it. Starting now.

• 항공운송 실무영어 Practical English for Cabin Crew

Key Vocabulary & Expressions

Word / Phrase	Meaning
seat pocket	the pouch on the back of the passenger seat
overhead bin	storage compartment above the seats
galley	kitchen area of the aircraft
inspect	examine carefully
suspicious	possibly dangerous or unusual

Alternative Expressions

Original	Alternative
Let's begin the post-flight cabin check.	Let's start inspecting the cabin after arrival.
Please start with the aft section.	Begin your check from the rear of the cabin.
Don't forget to inspect the lavatories.	Make sure to check the restrooms, too.
Report them immediately.	Notify me right away.
Starting now.	I'll begin right away.

Situation 2: Handling Lost and Found Items

Setting:
While inspecting the cabin after passenger disembarkation, a crew member finds a personal item left behind.
Characters:
- Cabin Crew Member
- Purser

Dialogue

Crew: I found a phone under seat 18A.
Purser: Thanks. Let's tag it and log it in the lost and found report.
Crew: Should I place it in the designated drawer?
Purser: Yes, and write down the seat number and time found.

Unit 12. Post-Flight Duties & Debriefing

Crew: Done. Hopefully, the passenger claims it soon.
Purser: If not, ground staff will take over.

Key Vocabulary & Expressions

Word / Phrase	Meaning
lost and found	a system for handling misplaced items
tag	attach a label with details
log	to record officially
designated	specifically assigned
drawer	a compartment for storing items

Alternative Expressions

Original	Alternative
I found a phone under seat 18A.	There's a phone left behind in seat 18A.
Let's tag it and log it.	Label it and record it in the system.
Should I place it in the drawer?	Do I store it in the secure compartment?
Write down the seat number.	Record the exact location.
Ground staff will take over.	Airport personnel will handle it.

Situation 3: Filing Post-flight Reports

Setting:
After all post-flight tasks are done, the purser completes the service and incident report to submit to the airline's operations team.

Characters:
- Purser
- Cabin Crew Member

Dialogue

Purser: Any issues to report from the flight?
Crew: One passenger requested medical attention after landing.

Purser: I'll include that in the incident report. Any service feedback?
Crew: A few passengers praised the meal service.
Purser: Great. I'll add that to the service comments section.
Crew: Need help submitting the report?
Purser: No, I've got it. Thanks.

Key Vocabulary & Expressions

Word / Phrase	Meaning
incident report	official record of an unusual event
service feedback	comments from passengers about service
submit	send officially
praised	gave positive remarks
comments section	part of a form for written opinions

Alternative Expressions

Original	Alternative
Any issues to report?	Did anything happen that needs to be documented?
I'll include that in the report.	I'll note it in the form.
A few passengers praised the meal service.	Some guests complimented the in-flight meals.
I'll add that to the service comments section.	I'll write that in the feedback area.
I've got it.	I can take care of it.

Situation 4: Crew Debriefing

Setting:
After landing and completing all post-flight tasks, the cabin crew gathers for a short debriefing. During the flight, there was an issue involving a difficult passenger who became upset during the meal service. The crew must discuss how it was handled and how to improve in the future.

 Unit 12. Post-Flight Duties & Debriefing

Characters:
- Purser
- Cabin Crew A (Main responder to passenger complaint)
- Cabin Crew B (Assisted during the situation)

Dialogue

Purser: Thank you for your efforts today. Let's go over any issues that came up during the flight.
Crew A: There was a situation with the passenger in 14C. He became upset when his meal choice was unavailable.
Purser: Yes, I was informed. How did you handle it?
Crew A: I apologized sincerely and explained the situation. I offered him the alternative meal and a beverage of choice.
Crew B: I also followed up with him mid-flight to ensure he was okay.
Purser: Good job on the follow-up. Was he calm afterward?
Crew A: He was still a bit frustrated but didn't cause further problems.
Purser: In the future, let's proactively inform passengers earlier when options are limited. Communication can help reduce frustration.
Crew A: Understood. I'll make sure to announce meal shortages earlier.
Purser: Great. Let's add this to our debriefing notes. Anything else?

Key Vocabulary & Expressions

Word / Phrase	Meaning
unavailable	not in stock or not provided
sincerely	honestly and with care
alternative meal	another option for food
follow-up	to check again after initial action
proactively	acting in advance to prevent problems

•항공운송 실무영어 Practical English for Cabin Crew

Alternative Expressions

Original Expression	Alternative Expression
Let's go over any issues.	Let's review any problems that occurred.
He became upset.	He got frustrated.
I apologized sincerely.	I gave a heartfelt apology.
I offered him the alternative meal.	I suggested another available option.
Let's add this to our debriefing notes.	Make sure this is recorded in today's review.

Comprehension Check

Instructions:

Answer the following questions based on the situation you studied.

1. Why did the passenger in 14C become upset?

a) His seat was broken

b) His meal choice was unavailable

c) His luggage was missing

d) The flight was delayed

2. How did Cabin Crew A respond to the passenger's complaint?

a) Ignored the passenger

b) Apologized and offered an alternative

c) Informed the purser immediately

d) Gave the passenger compensation

3. What additional step did Cabin Crew B take?

a) Brought a new meal

b) Escalated to the captain

c) Followed up with the passenger

d) Switched the passenger's seat

Unit 12. Post-Flight Duties & Debriefing

4. What suggestion did the Purser give for future flights?

a) Avoid meal service

b) Serve all passengers quickly

c) Inform passengers early about limited options

d) Assign seats according to meals

Wrap-up Quiz

Part 1. Word Match

Match each word with its correct definition.

Word	Meaning
1. Debriefing	a) A summary meeting to review the flight and crew performance
2. Lost and Found	b) Items left behind by passengers
3. Cabin Check	c) A document written after the flight to report incidents or issues
4. Report Filing	d) Final inspection of the cabin for safety and cleanliness

Part 2. Fill in the Blanks

Complete the sentences with the correct words from the box.

report	missing	personal
cabin	debriefing	lavatory

5. Cabin crew should check the _____ for any left-behind items.

6. A _____ is written when there is an in-flight incident.

7. Make sure no _____ items are left in the overhead bins.

8. We found a bag with _____ belongings in seat 14A.

9. The _____ after the flight helps improve future teamwork.

10. Check if the _____ is clean and properly stocked.

• 항공운송 실무영어 Practical English for Cabin Crew

Part 3. Short Answer

Answer in one or two full sentences.

11. What should cabin crew do if they find a lost item?

12. Why is the post-flight debriefing important for cabin crew?

Role-play Activity Worksheet

Objective:

Practice real-life communication scenarios that cabin crew may encounter after a flight. Improve your teamwork, problem-solving, and reporting skills.

Instructions:

- Form a group of 3.
- Assign roles: one Purser and two Cabin Crew Members.
- Choose a scenario provided on the worksheet (or assigned by your instructor).
- Review the setting and character roles.
- Understand the situation and think about what happened during the flight.
- Create a short dialogue (1.5-2 minutes) based on the given scenario.
- Include key actions, issues, communication, and resolution.
- Perform the role-play in front of your classmates or in your small group.
- After your role-play, complete the reflection section to think about what was done well and what can be improved.

Role-play Situations

Situation 1: Missing Passenger Item

Scenario:
After landing, a passenger in 22A reported that their tablet was missing from the seat pocket. Cabin Crew A spoke with the passenger, while Cabin Crew B conducted a quick check.

Key Points to Discuss:
- When did the passenger notice the item missing?
- What actions did the crew take immediately?
- How was the issue handled and documented?
- Could anything have prevented the situation?

Situation 2: Passenger Complaint about Service Attitude

Scenario:
A passenger in Business Class mentioned in a post-flight comment that one crew member was "cold and inattentive." Cabin Crew A served the passenger and Cabin Crew B observed the interaction.

Key Points to Discuss:
- Was the feedback accurate?
- What were the possible causes of the passenger's impression?
- How could the interaction have been improved?
- What can be learned from this experience?

Situation 3: Medical Assistance Miscommunication

Scenario:

During the flight, a passenger in 37C had a minor allergic reaction. Cabin Crew A provided assistance but did not immediately inform the purser. Cabin Crew B later updated the purser near landing.

Key Points to Discuss:
- Was there a breakdown in communication?
- Were protocols followed properly?
- How was the passenger cared for, and what was the outcome?
- What procedures should be reinforced?

Reflection Sheet

After the role-play, fill in the reflection below:

1. What was handled well during the situation?
✍ _____

2. What could have been improved?
✍ _____

3. What communication skills were used?
✍ _____

4. What would you do differently next time?
✍ _____

Answer Keys

Answer Keys

Unit 01.

Word & Phrases
passenger manifest
flight details
special handling passengers
cabin crew
flight crew
crew coordination
briefing
emergency exits
safety equipment
turbulence

Unit 02.

Warm-up Quiz
1. A
2. D
3. E
4. B
5. C

Word & Phrases
seatbelt
restricted
suspicious
emergency exits
lavatory
aisle
galley
safety card
overhead bins
safety equipment

Comprehension Check
1. b
2. b
3. c
4. "All checks completed." or "Cross-check complete."
5. Example Answer: Report it immediately to the Purser or supervisor before boarding begins.

Wrap-up Quiz
1. C
2. A
3. B
4. D
5. Captain
6. ready
7. wheelchair
8. disarmed

Unit 03.

Warm-up 1
airline
departure
passenger name
departure date

destination
flight number
gate number
boarding time

Word & Phrases
window seat
in the back
go through
cooperation
boarding pass
middle
aisle
step aside
cabin
recheck

Warm-up 3
1. check-in
2. hand-baggage
3. boarding pass
4. seat number
5. Seating arrangements
6. window seats
7. in advance
8. hand-baggage
9. overhead bins

Wrap-up Quiz
1. boarding pass
2. left-hand side
3. aisle
4. cooperation
5. galley

Part 2.
B → D → C → A → E

Unit 04.

Comprehension check
1. b
2. c
3. c
4. b
5. c

Wrap-up Quiz
1. boarding pass
2. assist
3. duplicate
4. verify
5. switch
6. condition
7. across
8. assigned
9. seat map
10. aisle

Unit 05.

Wrap-up Quiz
1. upright
2. cross-check
3. demonstration

4. stow
5. seatbelt
6. b
7. c
8. a
9. d
10. F
11. T
12. F
13. T
14. b
15. b
16. b

Unit 06.
Warm-up Quiz
1. b
2. c
3. d
4. stock list
5. trolley
6. pre-set tray
7. galley
8. secure

Comprehension Check
1. F
2. T
3. F
4. F
5. galley

6. availability
7. galley crew
8. secured
9. To ensure all required service items are present, safe, and properly stored, and to prevent delays or safety risks.
10. Service order (which section goes first) / Shortages or missing items

Unit 07.
Wrap-up Quiz
1. b
2. a
3. c

Comprehension Check
PART A
1. F
2. F
3. F
4. T
5. F

PART B
1. c
2. a
3. b
4. c
5. b

PART C

Sample Answers

I'm sorry, that option is no longer available. May I suggest another choice?

Thank you so much for your cooperation. We truly appreciate your kindness.

Check if the passenger's cup is empty and politely ask if they'd like more.

UNIT 08.

Warm-up Quiz

1. c
2. b
3. b
4. b
5. b

Word Match Activity

1. b
2. d
3. a
4. c
5. e
6. f
7. g
8. h
9. I
10. j

Comprehension Check

Part 1

1. c
2. b
3. c

Part 2.

4. overhead
5. warm or hot

Part 3.

a → 1
b → 2
c → 3
d → 4

Part 4.

6. (Example Answer)

"Of course. I can bring you a pillow and a blanket if you'd like."

Part 5.

1 → b
2 → c
3 → a
4 → d

Unit 09.

Warm-Up Quiz

Part 1

1. c

2. d
3. b

Part 2
1. b
2. c
3. e
4. d
5. a

Part 3
1. apologize
2. resolve
3. empathy
4. turbulence
5. inconvenience

Comprehension Check
1. b
2. c
3. b
4. c
5. b
6. functioning
7. bottle
8. purser
9. discreetly
10. available

Wrap-up Quiz
Part 1
1. b

2. c
3. a
4. d

Part 2
1. c
2. b

Part 3
1. apologize
2. patience
3. seatbelt

Unit 10.

Warm-Up Quiz
1. F
2. T
3. F
4. T
5. F

Comprehension Check
1. c
2. b
3. d
4. c
5. c

Wrap-up Quiz
Part 1
1. c

2. b

3. b

Part 2

1. b
2. c
3. a
4. d
5. e

Part 3

1. fasten
2. return
3. upright
4. tray
5. landing

Unit 11.

Warm-up Quiz

Part 1

1. B
2. D
3. E
4. C
5. A

Part 2

1. taxiing
2. disarm
3. security check
4. farewell greeting

5. transit passenger

Comprehension Check

1. b
2. c
3. c
4. c
5. c

Wrap-up Quiz

Part 1

1. c
2. c
3. b

Part 2

1. doors to arrival
2. seated
3. personal belongings

Part 3

A. 2
B. 3
C. 1

Unit 12.

Warm-up Quiz

Part 1

1. C
2. A
3. B

4. D
5. E

Part 2
6. cleaning crew
7. report
8. debriefing
9. cabin inspection
10. trash

Part 3
Short Answer(Sample Answers)
11. What should cabin crew check during the post-flight cabin inspection?
Check seat pockets, overhead bins, lavatories, and ensure no personal items or trash are left.

12. Why is the debriefing important after a flight?
To review the service, share feedback, and improve future performance.

Comprehension Check
1. b
2. b
3. c
4. c

Wrap-up Quiz
Part 1.
1. a
2. b
3. d
4. c

Part 2.
5. cabin
6. report
7. personal
8. missing
9. debriefing
10. lavatory

Part 3. Short Answer(Sample Answers)

11.
They should label the item, record the seat number or location, and hand it over to the Lost and Found department.

12.
It allows the team to review flight performance, share feedback, and improve future service quality.

에듀컨텐츠·휴피아
CH Educontents·Huepia

항공운송 실무영어
【 Practical English for Cabin Crew 】

2025년 11월 15일 초판 1쇄 인쇄
2025년 11월 20일 초판 1쇄 발행

| 저　　자 | 최 경 옥 · 지음 |

발 행 처	도서출판 에듀컨텐츠휴피아
발 행 인	李 相 烈
등록번호	제2017-000042호 (2002년 1월 9일 신고등록)
주　　소	서울 광진구 자양로 28길 98, 동양빌딩
전　　화	(02) 443-6366
팩　　스	(02) 443-6376
e-mail	iknowledge@naver.com
web	http://cafe.naver.com/eduhuepia
만든사람들	기획·김수아 / 책임편집·이진훈 정민경 김소현 디자인·유충현 / 영업·이순우

| I S B N | 978-89-6356-528-6 (13320) |
| 정　　가 | 15,000원 |

> 이 책은 저작권법에 따라 보호받는 저작물이므로 무단전재와 무단복제를 금지하며, 책 내용의 전부 또는 일부를 이용하려면 반드시 저작권자의 서면 동의를 받아야 합니다.